CAMBRIDGE LIBRARY COLLECTION

Books of enduring scholarly value

Latin American Studies

This series focuses on colonial Latin America and the Caribbean. It includes historical and statistical reference works from the eighteenth and nineteenth centuries, reports describing scientific, archaeological and ethnological expeditions, and editions of accounts from the earliest period of European settlement.

Haytian Papers

Prince Sanders (1775–1839) was an African-American teacher and advocate of black American emigration to Africa and Haiti. When Sanders was on a speaking tour of England he met abolitionist William Wilberforce, who encouraged him to go to Haiti and meet King Henri Christophe (1767–1820). Haiti during this time was divided, and Christophe ruled over the northern region. Sanders travelled to the island and was quickly hired as Christophe's adviser. In 1816 Sanders published this translation of documents, which include Christophe's land reforms, his establishment of a monarchy in Haiti, and some of his correspondence. This publication was part of an attempt by Christophe and Sanders to show white Europeans that former slaves could successfully run their own country without international interference. Although Haiti was reunited in 1820, after Christophe's death, these documents illustrate his efforts to protect the country during its fragile early years of independence.

Cambridge University Press has long been a pioneer in the reissuing of out-of-print titles from its own backlist, producing digital reprints of books that are still sought after by scholars and students but could not be reprinted economically using traditional technology. The Cambridge Library Collection extends this activity to a wider range of books which are still of importance to researchers and professionals, either for the source material they contain, or as landmarks in the history of their academic discipline.

Drawing from the world-renowned collections in the Cambridge University Library and other partner libraries, and guided by the advice of experts in each subject area, Cambridge University Press is using state-of-the-art scanning machines in its own Printing House to capture the content of each book selected for inclusion. The files are processed to give a consistently clear, crisp image, and the books finished to the high quality standard for which the Press is recognised around the world. The latest print-on-demand technology ensures that the books will remain available indefinitely, and that orders for single or multiple copies can quickly be supplied.

The Cambridge Library Collection brings back to life books of enduring scholarly value (including out-of-copyright works originally issued by other publishers) across a wide range of disciplines in the humanities and social sciences and in science and technology.

Haytian Papers

*A Collection of the Very
Interesting Proclamations,
and Other Official Documents*

Edited by Prince Sanders

CAMBRIDGE
UNIVERSITY PRESS

CAMBRIDGE UNIVERSITY PRESS

Cambridge, New York, Melbourne, Madrid, Cape Town,
Singapore, São Paolo, Delhi, Mexico City

Published in the United States of America by Cambridge University Press, New York

www.cambridge.org
Information on this title: www.cambridge.org/9781108050531

© in this compilation Cambridge University Press 2013

This edition first published 1816
This digitally printed version 2013

ISBN 978-1-108-05053-1 Paperback

By Authority.

HAYTIAN PAPERS.

A

COLLECTION

OF THE VERY

INTERESTING PROCLAMATIONS,

AND OTHER

OFFICIAL DOCUMENTS;

TOGETHER WITH

SOME ACCOUNT OF THE RISE, PROGRESS, AND
PRESENT STATE

OF

THE KINGDOM OF HAYTI.

WITH A PREFACE

BY

PRINCE SANDERS, ESQ.

AGENT FOR THE HAYTIAN GOVERNMENT.

LONDON:

PRINTED FOR W. REED, LAW BOOKSELLER,
NO. 17, FLEET STREET.

1816.

T. Bensley and Son,
Bolt Court, Fleet Street, London.

CONTENTS.

TO THE PUBLIC.

I AM induced to lay the following Transla-
tions of Haytian State Papers, in conjunction
with some extracts from their ordinary Publications, before the British people generally,
in order to give them some more correct information with respect to the enlightened sys-
tems of policy, the pacific spirit, the altogether
domestic views, and liberal principles of the
Government; and also to more obviously
evince the ameliorated and much improved
condition of all classes of society in that new
and truly interesting Empire (with which I
have the honour to be connected) than I am
inclined to think have hitherto been fully
known or understood in this country.

For I am deeply penetrated with the conviction, that it is only necessary that the actual character and feelings of the Haytians

should be made apparent, to most assuredly and most satisfactorily allay all those apprehensions of their interference with the internal regulations of neighbouring powers, which the enemies to the Abolition of the Slave Trade, and the foes to all attempts at the improvement and elevation of the African race, would, by their misrepresentations and false statements, endeavour to excite in the minds of this nation of genuine philanthropists. But to the immortal honour of noble and generous Englishmen be it said, their hearts are in general attuned to the exercise of more humane, and more rationally illumined views and sentiments. O happy England! to thee most appropriately belong the exalted appellations of protectress of the Christian world; the strong hold of rational freedom; the liberatress as well as the genuine asylum for oppressed humanity, and the promulgatress of civilization, knowledge, and piety to every region of the globe. In thee we see a practical exemplification of those principles of benevolence and kind affection which encompass the human character with an imperishable lustre of glory and honour.

Having understood that it has often been insinuated by those few individuals, whose habitual labour is the perversion, (and as far as they are able,) the absolute destruction of every object which has a tendency to show that the Blacks possess, to any considerable extent, that portion of natural intelligence which the beneficent Father of all ordinarily imparts to His children; I say, being convinced, that for these inglorious and malevolent purposes, such persons have endeavoured to impress the public with the idea, that those official documents which have occasionally, appeared in this country, are not written by black Haytians themselves ; but that they are either written by Europeans in this country, or by some who, *they say*, are employed for that purpose in the public offices at Hayti ; and, for the entire refutation of this gross misrepresentation, I upon my honour declare, that there is not a single white European at present employed in writing at any of the public offices; and that all the public documents are written by those of the King's Secretaries whose names they bear, and that they are all black men, or men of colour.

It is my humble, though sincere opinion, that no one can visit Hayti at this period, and have an opportunity of seeing the decency of manners, the apparent cheerfulness, the happiness and industry which prevail among all grades of the community, without being struck with the astonishing accuracy with which it has pleased God to bring to pass a state of society there, the very idea of the establishment of which in that country Mr. Bryan Edwards observed, in his History of St. Domingo, " is so pleasing to the imagination, that every humane and reflecting mind must wish it may be realized."

Says Mr. Edwards, " I might here expatiate upon the wonderful dispensations of Divine Providence in raising up enslaved Africans to avenge the wrongs of the injured Aborigines; I might also indulge the *fond* but *fallacious idea*, that, as the negroes of St. Domingo have been eye-witnesses of the benefits of civilized life among the whites; have seen in what manner and to what extent social order, sober industry, and submission to the laws, contribute to individual and general prosperity (advantages which were denied to them in their native country), some superior spirits may hereafter

rise up among them, by whose encouragement
and example they may be taught, in due time,
to discard the ferocious and sordid manners
and pursuits of savage life; to correct their
vices, and be led progressively on to civilization and gentleness, to the knowledge of
truth, and the practice of virtue!

" This picture (then continues he) is so
pleasing to the imagination, that every humane
and reflecting mind must wish it may be realized; but I am afraid it is the mere creation of
the fancy, the fabric of a vision !"

If it had pleased God to spare Mr. Edwards
to this time, and he had been permitted to re-
visit Hayti in its present improved state, I am
inclined to think he would be ready to exclaim,
" I now behold here a scene of things, the mo-
mentary anticipation of the possibility of the
existence of which among these people, a few
years since, seemed to me like the " mere
creation of the fancy," and the " fabric of a
vision."

They are now blest with a Sovereign, whose
sincere desire, and firmly settled purpose, most
obviously appears to be the elevation of the

characters, and the improvement of the hearts
and lives, of all the various classes of society.
It especially appears to be his object to ame-
liorate the condition and improve the character
of the humblest class, namely, that of the
plantation labourers. For the full confirmation
of the truth of this fact, the following extracts
from the laws relating to the agricultural interest, and management in all its relative de-
partments and bearings, will be most satisfactory to every reflecting and unprejudiced
mind.

P. SANDERS.

CODE HENRI.

LAW RESPECTING THE CULTURE.

Titre 1, *Chap.* 1.

The proprietors and farmers of land are bound to treat their respective labourers with true paternal solicitude; an obligation which it is greatly for their own interest to fulfil in its utmost extent.

2 Chap. 16 *par. Page 5.*

The law exacts from the labourers in return a reciprocal attention to the welfare and interest of the landlord and farmer.

Titre 4, *Pa. 56.*

In lieu of wages, the labourers in plantations shall be allowed a full fourth of the gross product, free from all duties and expenses to the time of removal.

Page 1, Art. I. It is the King's express order, that on every complaint of the cultivators against their landlords and farmers, the lieutenant commanding in the parish shall immediately attend to the circumstances of the case; and on proof of the grievance, report to the the general of the district, who shall thereupon transmit the same to the privy council, who shall decide on the case, and pronounce sentence of punishment according to the nature of the offence.

On refusal of this parish officer to enter into the business, the plaintiff is authorised to address the commandant; in default of whose interference he may address the general of division; and, if need be, the privy council direct.

III. No landlord or farmer has authority to reject any cultivator from his habitation on pretext of illness or infirmity.

IV. An hospital shall be built on every plantation wherein the sick labourers shall be attended by professional assistance, and supplied with medicines at the expense of the landlord or farmer, who is to secure the personal attendance twice in each week.

Another hospital shall be provided for such as are afflicted with contagious disorders.

Independent of the professional visitor, each hospital shall be provided with a midwife and a female nurse.

V. The medical visitors are bound to act in conformity with all the King's ordinances respecting the exercise of their profession.

VI. Landlords and proprietors are bound to maintain and support the aged and infirm cultivators, and to furnish medicine and attendance.

VII. Landlords and farmers are most expressly prohibited from forcing their cultivators to quit their dwellings for the purpose of working at another plantation, or in any other branch of cultivation than that in which they have been accustomed to labour, without the privy council's permission; to be obtained only on proof of the lands proposed to be abandoned being no longer susceptible of production.

VIII. Resident planters convicted of having suborned or connived at the desertion of a soldier, or his absence without a furlough, are punishable according to art. 12. sect. 2. of the military code.

IX. Farmers are obliged to furnish tools and implements of cultivation, for which the managers shall be responsible.

X. Provision grounds shall be allotted upon every plantation in presence of the public authorities, and proportionally among the respective labouring families, according to the quality and extent of the land applicable to such purpose.

XI. In case of fire, the labourers on contiguous plantations are enjoined to assist in extinguishing it, and the neighbouring farmers to contribute in every way to that effect.

XII. No landlord or cultivator shall carry fire among the cane-pieces, nor plant any fresh wood upon his boundaries without due notice to his neighbour, and observation of the distances proper, to prevent accidents by fire.

XIII. Farmers have the right of pasturing their saddle and carriage horses: but the attendants of these animals shall have no right to share in the crop.

XIV. The keep of too many animals upon cultivated land being found prejudicial to cultivation and good husbandry, their number shall be limited, and the surplus number turned into the common field.

XV. A limited number of attendants on the plantation cattle shall share in the fourth part of the produce allotted to the agriculturists and assistants in the manufacture.

Chap. II.

Art. XVII. The law punishes the lazy and vagabond, among whom are comprehended labourers of both sexes who shall quit the habitations in which they have domiciled, in order to reside in towns or other places where they are forbidden to settle: penalty, Art. 114. Titre 8.

XVIII. Marriage being the source of moral conduct, it shall be especially encouraged and protected; and the laborious peasantry who shall bring up the greatest number of legitimate children in a reputable manner, shall be distinguished and encouraged by government itself.

XIX. Mendicity and female licentiousness are severely reprobatedall; beggars on the highway, prostitutes, and stragglers shall be arrested, and such as have no legal settlement placed by the proper authorities, in their discretion, to labour for their livelihood. His Majesty's governors and lieutenants are strictly ordered to enforce these regulations, and the good and faithful subjects invited to denounce the delinquents.

XX. Every conductor or manager who shall be convicted of neglecting the cultivation confided to his care, or of converting to his own benefit the property of his employer, by diverting the workmen to fish or chase, employ them in building for his own benefit, or who shall have mistreated the labourers, or misused his own authority, shall be liable to the penalties in Art. 115. T. 111.

XXI. The misconduct of managers and conductors with respect to others, in which the proprietors and farmers appear neither to have participated nor to have derived any advantage, shall in no case attach to the latter, nor to prejudice the interest of absentees: but if the case be otherwise, they shall be responsible according to the nature of the transaction.

XXII. The following hours of labour are irrevocably established.

Work shall commence with the day-light, and be continued uninterruptedly till eight o'clock:—one hour is allotted to the labourer for breakfast on the spot where employed; at nine work recommences until noon, when two hours repose are granted them : at two exactly they recommence work, and shall not leave off before night-fall.

XXIII. Women pregnant, or with children at nurse, are exempt from field labour.

XXIV. Prayers shall be read to the labourers every night, and the landlord, farmer, or manager, shall invite the people to attend on the Sabbath and on fast days to public prayers in their parish.

XXV. Proprietors, farmers, and managers of plantations are compelled to see the provision-ground well kept by the respective labourers to whom they have been granted : if the latter neglect this duty, they shall be employed in it

during their hours of respite from plantation-
work.

XXVI. No labourer, without permission of
the lieutenant of the King, shall absent himself
from the plantation on working days, unless
this be obtained through the overseer or conductor.

XXVII. On the appearance of disorder or
seditious movement on a plantation, the proprie-
tor, farmer, or superintendant, shall apply to his
neighbours for assistance in arresting the
guilty; after which notice shall be dispatched
to the commandant of the police, who is bound
to repair to the spot and secure the disturbers
of the public peace, imprison, and report to the
proper authorities, on pain of becoming per-
sonally liable for all consequences.

———

I would here beg leave to observe, that
while reading the foregoing laws, in order to
have a fair understanding of the grounds upon
which the military aspect of them is to be
justly founded and approved, is, that at the
period when they were framed the whole popu-

lation were soldiers ; and all the most improved and intelligent men were placed in the highest civil and military offices: in this state of things, a government bearing some degree of consonance to the condition, character, wants, and employment of the whole people, was absolutely necessary.

P. S.

Extracts from the Registers of the Delibe-
rations of the Consuls of the Republic.

Nº I.

PARIS, 17th Brumaire,
in the 10th year of the French Republic,
one and indivisible.

Proclamation of the First Consul to the In-
habitants of St. Domingo.

WHATEVER be your origin or your colour, you are all Frenchmen, *you are all*
free and all equal before God, and before
the Republic.

France, as well as St. Domingo, has
been the prey of factions, dismembered
by civil and by foreign wars; but all is

B

changed. All nations have embraced the French, and sworn to them peace and amity. Frenchmen, too, have embraced one another, and have sworn unanimously to live as friends and brothers; come you, likewise, to throw yourselves into the arms of France, and rejoice to see once more your friends and brothers of Europe.

The government sends you the Captain-General *Leclerc*; he takes with him a numerous force for your protection against your enemies, and against the enemies of the Republic. Should any one whisper in your ear, " *These forces are destined to despoil you of your liberty ;*" answer, " *It is the Republic that has given us liberty ; the Republic will never suffer it to be ravished from us.*"

Rally around the Captain-General, he brings you back peace and plenty. Rally all around him : whoso dares to separate himself from the Captain-General shall be accounted a traitor to his country, and the wrath of the Republic shall devour him as fire devours your parched sugar canes.

Given at Paris, at the Palace of Government, the 17th Brumaire, in the 10th year of the French Republic.

(Signed)   BONAPARTE.

By the First Consul,

(Signed)   H. B. MARET, Secretary of State.

(A True Copy.)

(Signed)   LECLERC, Captain-General.

(A True Copy.)

(Signed)   The General, Chief of the Etat Major of the Army,

DUGUA.

N° II.

LIBERTY <small>AND</small> EQUALITY.

ARMY OF ST. DOMINGO.

Head Quarters on Board the Ocean,
13th Pluviose, 10th year of the Republic.

The General in Chief of the Army of St. Domingo, Captain-General of the Colony, to the General of Brigade, CHRISTOPHE, Commandant at the Cape.

I LEARN with indignation, Citizen General, that you refuse to receive the French squadron, and the French army that I command, under the pretext that you have received no orders from the Governor-General.

France has concluded a peace with England, and its government sends to St.

Domingo forces capable of subduing the rebels; at least if any are to be found at St. Domingo. As to you, General, I confess it will grieve me to account you among them.

I give you notice, that if you have not in the course of this day surrendered the Forts Picolet and Belair, with all the batteries on the coast, to-morrow, at daybreak, fifteen thousand troops shall be disembarked.

Four thousand men are, at this moment, landing at Fort Liberté; eight thousand more at Port Republican.

Herewith you will receive my Proclamation, which expresses the intentions of the French Government; but, recollect, whatever individual esteem your conduct in the colony may have inspired me with, I hold you responsible for what may happen.

I salute you.

(Signed)   LECLERC.

N° III.

Head-Quarters at the Cape,
13th Pluviose, year 10.

Henry Christophe, General of Brigade, Commandant of the Arrondissement of the Cape, to the General in Chief, Leclerc.

YOUR Aid-de-Camp, General, has delivered to me your letter of this day; I have the honour to inform you that I could not deliver up the forts and post confided to my command, without previous orders from the Governor-General, Toussaint Louverture, my immediate chief, from whom I hold the powers with which I am invested. I am fully persuaded that I have to do with Frenchmen, and that you are the chief of the armament called the expedition; but I wait the orders of the Governor, to whom I have dispatched one of my Aid-de-Camps, to apprize him of your arrival, and that of the French army, and cannot permit you to land until I have received his answer. If you put in force your threats of hostility, I shall make the resistance which becomes a general officer; and, should the chance of war be yours, you shall not enter Cape Town till it be reduced to ashes, nay, even in the ruins will I renew the combat.

You say that the French Government has sent to St. Domingo forces capable of subduing the rebels, if any such be found; it is your coming, and the hostile intentions you manifest, that alone could create them among a peaceable people, in perfect submission to France. The very mention of rebellion is an argument for our resistance.

As to the troops which you say are this moment landing, I consider them as so many pieces of cards which the least breath of wind will dissipate.

How can you hold me responsible for the event? You are not my Chief; I know you not, and can therefore make no account of you till you are recognised by Governor Toussaint.

For the loss of your esteem, General, I assure you that I desire not to earn it at the price that you set upon it, since to purchase it I must be guilty of a breach of duty.

I have the honour to salute you.

(Signed)   H. Christophe.

Nº IV.

Head Quarters at the Cape, 29th Germinal,
Year 10 of the French Republic.

The General in Chief to General Christophe.

You may give credit, Citizen General, to all that Citizen Vilton has written to you on behalf of General Hardy ; I will keep the promises which have been made you ; but, if it is your intention to submit to the Republic, think on the essential service you could render her by furnishing the means to secure the person of General Toussaint.

(Signed)   Leclerc.

Nº V.

The General of Brigade, Henry Christophe,
to General Leclerc.

I HAVE received yours of the 29th of
last month. With earnest desire to give
credit to what Citizen Vilton has written
me, I wait only for a proof which must
convince me of the intention to procure
the liberty and equality of the population
of this colony. The laws which consecrate
the principles, and which the mother
country, without doubt, has enacted, will
carry to my heart this conviction; and I
protest, that on obtaining this desired
proof, by being made acquainted with
these laws, I shall submit immediately.

You propose to me, Citizen General,
to furnish you with the means of securing

the person of General Toussaint Louverture. It would be perfidy and treason in me to do so, and a proposition so degrading to me, is, in my opinion, a mark of your invincible repugnance to believe me susceptible of the smallest sentiment of delicacy and honour. He is my commander, and my friend. Is friendship, Citizen General, compatible with such monstrous baseness?

The laws which I have just mentioned, have been promised us, by the mother country, by the proclamation that her Consuls have addressed to us when they communicated the constitution of the 8th year. Fulfil, Citizen General, fulfil this maternal promise, by unfolding to our view the code which contains it, and you will soon behold all her children rushing into the arms of that beneficent mother, and amongst them General Toussaint Louverture, who, thus undeceived, like the rest, will hasten to correct his error. It is

only when this error shall have been so
dispelled, that, if he persist in spite of evidence, he can fairly be regarded as criminal, and be the first object of the ana-
thema you have launched against him,
and the measure you propose to me to
execute.

Consider, Citizen General, the happy
effects that will result from the mere publication of these laws to a people crushed,
of old, beneath the weight of burden, and
lacerated by the scourges of a barbarous
slavery, in whom the apprehension of
similar enormities is, doubtless, excusable:
a people, in short, who have tasted the
sweets of liberty and equality, and covet
no happiness beyond the assurance of
never more having to dread the fetters they
have broken. The exposure of these laws
before their eyes, will stop the effusion of
French blood by the hands of Frenchmen;
will restore to the Republic children who
may yet do her service; and, after the

horrors of civil war, bring back tranquillity, peace, and prosperity, to the bosom of this unhappy colony. The object is, without question, worthy of the greatness of the mother country: its attainment, Citizen General, would cover you with glory, with the blessings of a people who will take pleasure in forgetting the evils that they have suffered by the delay of this promulgation. Reflect, that to refuse them a participation of these laws, so necessary for the salvation of these countries, would be to perpetuate those evils, and must lead to absolute destruction. In the name of my country, in the name of the mother country, I call for these salutary laws. Produce them, and St. Domingo is saved.

I have the honour to salute you.

(Signed)   H. Christophe.

N° VI.

ARMY OF THE EXPEDITION.

Head Quarters at the Cape, the 4th Floreal,
Year 10 of the French Republic.

The General in Chief to General Christophe.

I HAVE just received your letter, General : the uneasiness you testify to me is of a nature easy to be removed. You demand of me the code which gives assurance of liberty to the Negroes ; that code is not completed : I am engaged upon it at this moment. The wisdom of the First Consul did not allow him to make a code for the government of a country with which he was unacquainted, and of which the accounts he has received are contradictory ; but I declare to you in the presence of the colony ; I protest before the Supreme Being, whose assistance is never invoked in vain, that the bases of this code are, liberty and equality; that the Negroes shall be free ; and that the system of cultivation shall be founded upon the basis of that of General Toussaint, which may perhaps be even ameliorated in their favour. If this declaration is insufficient, it will be to me a convincing proof, that you have no wish to submit to the Republic. If it be sufficient, present yourself to-morrow at the village of Cape Heights ; I shall be there, and I declare to you, that if, after an hour's explanation, we do not come to a proper understanding, you shall be at liberty to return to your troops, upon the word of honour of the General in Chief.

What I have said to you on the subject of General Toussaint, arose from my not supposing him to be actuated by such loyal views as yourself. I shall take pleasure in finding myself deceived ; the answer you have made, on this head, gave me great satisfaction, and confirms me in the opinion I have always had of your loyalty.

If you come, and we understand each other, the war will have lasted so much shorter time in the colony. If not, calculate my means and your chances of successful resistance.

I salute you.

(Signed)   LECLERC.

Let me know the result of your arrangements, for I intend to absent myself from the Cape for some moments.

(Signed)   LECLERC.

N° VII.

LIBERTY AND EQUALITY.

Head Quarters, Cardineau, Grande Riviere,
5 Floreal, Year 10.

The General of Brigade, Henry Christophe,
to General Leclerc.

I THIS moment received your letter of yesterday : its contents revive in my mind the hope of seeing tranquillity, peace, and prosperity, returned to this too-long agitated colony, under the auspices of liberty and equality. I accept your offer of an interview ; to-morrow, at eleven o'clock in the morning, I shall present myself at Cape Heights, to confer with you. The word of a French General is, in my estimation, too sacred and inviolable to be denied belief.

C

I am flattered with the opinion you entertain of my loyalty ; but regret that you still persist in thinking General Toussaint uninspired by that estimable feeling ; give me leave to say, that you are deceived with regard to him. I have no apprehensions of finding myself deceived, when I assure you, that the confirmation of civilized liberty and equality will make him throw himself into the arms of the Republic.

It is hopeless to enter upon any calculation of our respective means ; the resolution to be a man, and a free man, is the unit of my arithmetic ; and the certainty of seeing this title insured to my fellow-citizens, will soon resolve our divided forces into one and the same body, into one and the same family, united by the sincerest fraternity.

I have the honour, &c.
(Signed)   H. CHRISTOPHE.

N° VIII.

Head Quarters at the Cape,
8th Floreal, Year 10.

The General in Chief to the General of Brigade, Christophe, commandant of the Cordon of the North.

I APPROVE, Citizen General, of the motives which prevent your presence at the Cape to-day. I am the more gratified by your effecting this operation in person, because the execution of your orders experienced some difficulties at Limbé.

The commandant, Lafleur, who occupies the great cut of Limbé, would not consent to surrender his post without having seen you. It appears that the same thing has taken place on the side of the landing-place of Limbé. General Salme had sent troops to occupy these posts; on the refusal to surrender them, the troops retired. Some mounted dragoons of the country, and some of the rustic militia, came to his camp to buy provisions. General Salme caused them to be disarmed and sent back. I have given orders for their arms to be restored.

As soon as you have completed the arrangements on the side of Grande Rivière, proceed to the crossway of Limbé, where you will find General Salme, who commands the arrondissement de Plaisance, and all the country that lies beyond the Rivière Salée. Take measures, in consulting with him, so that he may forthwith occupy the military posts at present in charge of your troops, and give orders that the rustic militia retire immediately to their habitations.—Put in requisition every possible means of conveyance, in order to facilitate the provisioning of the troops cantoned in the mountains.

I salute you.

(Signed) LECLERC.

As soon as you have concluded the business at Limbé, you will come and join me.

(Signed) LECLERC.

N° IX.

LIBERTY   AND   EQUALITY.

Head Quarters of the Cape, 30th Germinal,
Year 10 of the French Republic.

The General of Division Hardy, command-
ing the division of the North at St. Do-
mingo, to General Christophe, command-
ing the Cordon of the North.

CAPTAIN VILTON, in command at
the Petit Anse, has communicated to me,
Citizen General, the letter which you
have written to him, and I imparted it
immediately to the general in chief, Leclerc.

By the details into which you have
entered with Citizen Vilton, it is easy to
discover, General, that you have been
the victim of the treacherous insinuations
of an infinity of beings who, during the

course of the revolution in France, have set all parties on fire together ; have every where excited trouble and discord ; and who, after having brought upon themselves their own expulsion, have taken refuge in this colony, where they have distorted every fact and circumstance, disseminated the most atrocious falsehoods and calumnies, and sought, in fresh troubles, an existence that they could no longer find in Europe.

These crafty men have inspired you with distrust of the French government and its delegates. The conduct of the government and its good faith are well known to the whole world. Our own behaviour, since our arrival in St. Domingo, our proceedings towards the peaceable inhabitants, and in the instances of Generals Clervaux, Paul Louverture, Maurepas, Laplume, and their companions in arms, may give you a just measure of all that malevolence and intrigue have invented to slander the purity of our intentions.

Twelve years, General, have we been fighting for liberty; can you believe that, after such great sacrifices, we would so degrade ourselves in our own eyes as to incur a blemish which would efface our glory and destroy our work? Return, General, to more reasonable sentiments, and assure yourself, that your principles are ours also.

The reputation you enjoy in this country led us not to presume, that the French, your brothers, would encounter any resistance in you to the will of the government.

Nevertheless, General, all hope of obtaining from this same government oblivion of the past is not entirely lost to you. I address you with the frankness of a soldier, unacquainted with shifts and evasions.—Correct your errors; your return to true principles may accelerate the reparation of evils which have afflicted this beautiful spot. It is unworthy of you to serve as a stepping-stone to an usurper, to a rebel. The mother country throws wide her arms to all her children led astray, and invites them to take refuge in her bosom.

If you have a serious intention of recognizing the laws of the republic, and of submitting to the orders of her government, you will not hesitate, General, to come and join us with your troops. Hitherto we have fought you as enemies; tomorrow, if you will, we will embrace you as brothers.

Write me your proposals, or inform me at what hour you will be at Vaudreuil, to make them verbally. You will find me there. If we do not come to an understanding, I give you my word of honour, after the conference, you shall be at liberty to return to your head quarters.

I have the honour to salute you.

(Signed)   HARDY.

N° X.

Head Quarters, Robillard, Grand Boucan,
2d Floreal, Year 10.

*The General of Brigade, Henry Christophe,
to the General of Division, Hardy.*

Your letter of the 30th Germinal
has reached me. You are wrong in believing me the victim of the machinations
of perfidious intriguers. Nature, without
having endued me with all the subtlety of
a penetrating and clear-sighted genius, has
furnished me with sense enough to guard
me from the insinuations of wicked men.
With an ardent love of peace and tranquillity, I have always kept at a distance
from me violent and turbulent men, whose
empoisoned breath engenders confusion
and discord ; but I have not been exempt

from the suspicions that so many publications have roused in my mind, and which so many others have confirmed. Some originated in foreign countries, others in the heart of France. All announced, with a menacing tone, the misfortunes which now afflict us. How happens it, that the desires of the wicked, and the predictions of the evil-minded, appear so much in unison with the resolutions of the mother country?

When we were thus threatened with the return of slavery, after having broken its fetters, was any thing more natural than the dread of its return ; than the suspicion, the restlessness, even the mistrust of a people so often deceived ; so constantly the mark for the declared hatred of the enemies of its liberty, who were jealous of the equality admitted in their favour? Could we be otherwise, when every thing concurred to justify our fears?

General, we too have twelve years

combated for liberty, for the same rights,
which, like yourselves, we bought at the
price of our blood ; and I have ever revolted at the belief that the French, after
having made such sacrifices to obtain
them, would one day come to tear them
from a people who glory in being a part
of the great nation, and in enjoying in
common with her the advantages derived
from the revolution. That revolution, and
the benefits it has diffused, are worthy of
the glory of the Republic ; and when you
assure me, that she will not destroy her
work, why refuse to this branch of her family what must infallibly consolidate and
immortalize for her the sublime edifice!
The code of laws, promised to the inhabitants of the colonies by the proclamation of the consuls which accompanied
their communication of the constitution
of the year 8, can alone convey to my
mind the pledge of the consolidation of
our rights. This, Citizen General, is the

only weapon capable of subduing the apprehensions of a justly suspicious people! This a convincing proof, which alone can restore in my mind these sentiments to which you would recall me, and assure me that our mutual principles are the same!

The candour with which you address me is worthy, in all respects, of a soldier like yourself; I express myself with equal frankness ; and if General Leclerc, instead of proposing to me an act of treason and infamy, which would degrade me in my own eyes, had spoken to me as you have done, a language consistent with sentiments of honour and delicacy, such as he might fairly have presumed in me, I should have at least consented to the interview which you invite, not only at Vaudreuil, but at Le Petit Anse, or even at the Cape. But, be it as it may, I augur too favourably of your frankness and your word of honour, not to consent to that interview; not at the place you point out, but at one which may be near the centre of our respective lines. I therefore propose the house of Montalibor for this purpose. If that is agreeable to you, appoint the day and hour when you will meet me there, and I promise to be present. But, General, furnish yourself with the code of laws which are to govern this country, which confirm liberty and equality to the people who will water and fertilize it with their sweat, and our interview will be crowned with the happiest success, and I rejoice to owe to you the information which can alone dispel our error. Doubt not, General, that General Toussaint Louverture himself, whom General Leclerc considers but as a criminal, will then not hesitate to throw himself, with the whole nation, into the arms of the Republic, and, reunited under the auspices of these beneficent laws, this grateful people will offer him again, as a proof of their devotion, the exertions that they have once before directed to render this portion of the French Empire productive.

I have the honour, &c.

(Signed)   H. CHRISTOPHE.

N° XI.

Petit Anse, 26th Germinal, year 10.

Vilton, Commandant of the Petit Anse, to Citizen Henry Christophe, General of Brigade, at his Head-Quarters.*

MY DEAR COMRADE,

I GIVE way to the sentiments that my ancient friendship inspires for you;

* The two letters subjoined under the signature of Sieur Vilton, were fabricated by the Sieur Anquetil, who wrote them with his own hand at the house of

I have heard with the deepest regret your refusal to submit to the will of the French general whom the First Consul has dispatched to St. Domingo, to complete, support, and consolidate the order that you had so effectually established at the Cape Town, the dependance of the north, where you acquired the regard and affection of all the colonists. You repeatedly told me, my dear Comrade, that your greatest pleasure would be to see the French arrive, and resign into their hands the authority with which you were invested; by what fatality can you so suddenly have changed your good intentions? By this step you have renounced personal happiness, the security of your fortune, and the splendid establishment you could have secured to your amiable fa-

the Sieur Blin de Villeneuve, one of the great planters of the northern district, grandfather to the Sieur Vilton, who had no hand in them but the signature, to which he was forced by the French government.

mily; you have plunged them, as well as yourself, into the most frightful misery. Your intentions have always, to me, appeared so pure, and your devotion to the French nation left me nothing to doubt on the conduct you purposed to pursue; when, in an instant, upon the appearance of the French squadron you were no longer the same man. All the world, and your friends in particular, were persuaded that you had been ill-advised, and perhaps overruled by some black chiefs which were about you. So many handsome things have been said of you to M. Leclerc, the general in chief, that he is thoroughly convinced that it is owing to evil counsels that you took the resolution to resist; that he is ready to pardon you if you will reduce to obedience the troops that you command, and surrender the post that you occupy. This is a fine opening, my dear Comrade, for yourself, as well as the brave officers and soldiers

D

under your command ; they will be all
treated in the same manner as the French
army, and you will secure for yourself and
family every happiness that you can desire; especially if you should desire to
quit the colony, which is the best course
you can take to save yourself from being
exposed to the hatred of the rebels to
the orders of France, who shall refuse to
follow your example; you will be certain
of a liberal fortune, and may enjoy it
peaceably, under the protection of France,
in the country of your choice. My dear
Comrade, my tender friendship for you
and your family induces me to write this.
I shall partake of your happiness if I can
contribute to *effect it*. It lies with you to
give me this gratification by following the
advice of your old friend. Reply to me,
and let me know your intentions, that I
may bring them to bear in the way most
agreeable to yourself.

Every one here, and in all parts of

the colony, has witnessed the frankness
and good faith of the French generals,
and I have no reserve in repeating to you
the assurance that you may place entire
confidence in them; they will open to you
every facility, assist you with every means
in their power, and furnish you the con-
venience of carrying along with you every
thing you possess, and enjoying it peaceably wherever you choose. Trust me then,
my dear Comrade; quit this wandering
and vagabond life, which would disho-
nour you if you continue to follow it, and
regain the esteem of all good citizens, by
being yourself again, and abandoning the
cause of an ambitious man, who will be
your ruin in the end. Pay no regard to
your outlawry; the General in Chief, Leclerc, has said that it should not have
taken place had he known you sooner,
and that the Proclamation should be an-
nulled as soon as he learns that you have

acknowledged your error, and abandoned the cause of rebellion.

Health and Friendship.

(Signed)   VILTON.

N° XII.

Head Quarters, Hamlet of Dondon,
20th Germinal, year 10.

*The General of Brigade, Henry Christophe,
to the Commandant Vilton.*

I LOVE to give credit to the expressions of your long standing friendship for me, which has inspired you with the idea of addressing to me your letter of the 26th of this month. The sentiments of friendship I have avowed to you remain unalterable; you know me too well to doubt it.

Should I ever have refused to submit to the orders of the French general sent to this island by the First Consul of the Republic, if every thing had not conspired to convince me that the meditated consolidation of the good order which reigned in this colony, was nothing less than the destruction of our liberty, and the rights resulting from equality? It is true, as you say, I have declared my greatest desire was to see the French arrive, and to deposit in their hands the share of authority with which I was invested, and enjoy as a simple citizen the benefits of liberty and equality in the bosom of my family, in the midst of my fellow-citizens, provided that they too partook, with myself, of these sacred rights. A Frenchman, loving and respecting France, I joyfully entertained this hope, a hope that my confidence in the government of the mother country fostered and confirmed from day to day. I have never changed my in-

clinations in this respect; but by what
fatality is it that this hope has been deceived, that all has concurred to prove
that the principles previously adopted in
our favour have been changed? St. Domingo, wholly French, enjoyed, as you
know, the profoundest tranquillity; there
were no rebels to be found: by what
fatal blindness, then, did it happen, that
France has come with all the terrors of
war and the artillery of destruction? Not
to subdue the rebels (for rebels there were
none), but to create them amongst a peaceable people, and furnish a pretext to destroy or enslave them.

You say I have renounced my happiness. Alas! what happiness, what fortune,
what splendid establishment, of myself and
my family, could ever have offered me
consolation for the grief of seeing my fel-
lows reduced to the last degree of misfortune beneath the burthen of slavery? My
intentions have always been pure, and you

were, more than any body, acquainted
with my devotion to the French nation.
My intentions, my sentiments, have never
varied ; I have always been the same
man. But, placed as I was, by my fellow
citizens, as a sentinel at the post where it
was my duty to watch over the preservation of liberty, more dear to them than
their existence, how could I do otherwise
than alarm them at the approach of the
blow aimed at its annihilation ?

How many letters, pouring in upon
us in shiploads from France and foreign
countries, written in a menacing tone, by
colonists to other colonists, who preached
forth their contents with undisguised and
seditious vehemence, announced to me, in
the most explicit terms, the fate reserved
for the people of this colony and its defenders !

You know it. I have communicated
to several. Did I not, from motives of

prudence, conceal them from the governor, for fear of agitating him ; and did not my confidence in the government of the Republic so master my common sense as to make me, to the last moment, consider these letters as the mere expressions of the hatred of some wretches, who sought, in pure despite, again to embroil this country? Yet has not the event, notwithstanding my credulity, fully justified all their annunciations? The world, above all, my friends most especially, deceive themselves if they believe that I have allowed myself to be led away by any chiefs that are about me. At my age I have no need of counsel ; it is my duty that is my counsellor upon all occasions. You ought to know me better, and to be aware, that I never took advice of my friends, not even of you, whom I distinguished amongst them. Friends, alas! I thought I could count many ; but now, like Diogenes, with a lantern in my hand, at noon day, I search in vain for one upon whom I can rely.

It is without doubt very flattering to have so much good said of me to M. Leclerc, the general in chief; but he is wrong in persuading himself that my present conduct is the result of evil counsel. What I have said to you on that head is a complete answer to that opinion. I never had any intention of resisting him; and so I wrote word when he first appeared before the Cape; I testified to him how much regret I should feel if compelled to oppose reluctant resistance before receiving the orders of the chief who had placed me at this post, and who had intrusted me with a charge I could resign into no other hands. I sent to him Citizen Granier, commander of a battalion of the national guard, as the bearer of my letter, and charged him to express verbally the necessity I was under of waiting the orders

I expected from the governor, and my
resolution, when he should have been apprised of the squadron's arrival, to fulfil
the obligation of receiving it with all the
respect due to the mother country, in case
the governor, after being certified that it
was from France, should meditate resistance. Without attending to this reasonable observation, General Leclerc sends
back the Citizen Granier without any other
answer than this : " *That he had orders to
use force, and would execute them.*" A
trifling delay would have prevented much
calamity. As a man of honour, I was
determined to observe, religiously, what I
had charged the citizen Granier to represent on my behalf to General Leclerc :
but this general did not condescend to
give it credit; and, notwithstanding the
protestations he received of my devotion
to France, the port captain, whom I had
sent to meet the squadron, is still detained
on board, and his aid-de-camp forewarns

me, that if I send my adjutant general, he will be similarly treated. At the same time General Rochambeau effects a landing near Fort Liberty, without giving notice to the commander of that place, marches upon the forts which defend it, makes himself master of them, and puts to the sword the brave men he finds there, whilst the vessels enter the harbour, and discharge their guns upon the town. On the other hand, another landing is made at Limbé, which is likewise cannonaded, and the cape is placed between two numerous armies, with a menacing squadron in front. The terms of the letter which General Leclerc had addressed to me, showed plainly enough the object he had in view. I take counsel of the emergency of the circumstance in which I was placed by the conduct of this general; I take counsel, I say, of his own behaviour, and thus commence all the evils that afflict us.

After acting in such a manner, what

must not I suspect? Had I not reason to presume unfavourably, from the measures just put in execution against me? Yes I avow it; however great had been at all times my confidence in the French Government, I felt it powerfully shaken by the thundering threats, by the blows aimed at us, and the conduct of the chiefs of the French army determined mine.

You speak to me of fortune; I have no longer any; I have lost all. Honour is, henceforth, the only possession which is left to me and my family. You know me, and you know whether or not it is the object of my ambition.

You counsel me to make bold to ask permission to quit the colony. You cannot be ignorant that I am not deficient in courage, and in this case it would not fail me. I had resolved long since to quit the colony on the restoration of peace, and Citizen Granier was half inclined to the same course. If he exists, he can testify

to the truth of this assertion. My attachment to France had made me choose her
bosom as the asylum whither we might,
with our united families, have retired, and
passed our days in peace, in the sweet
certainty of leaving all our brethren free
and happy on the soil of this colony.
Why has every thing concurred to frus-
trate this hope? I expect to receive every
day the blow that will annihilate me; and
Citizen Granier, who, I learn, is detained
on board, has, perhaps, already ceased to
exist. What is his crime? What harm has
he done? Is it possible that his friendship
for me has been his crime?

You take upon yourself, my dear Comrade, to give me proofs of good faith and
frankness on the part of the French
Generals; you know not how it grieves
me to be unable to remove the just suspicion with which all the facts I have de-
tailed have inspired me; facts against
which I can find no reasonable or prudent

pretext for shutting my eyes. Happen what may, honour is my guide; and it is with extreme repugnance that I impute to any other rule of conduct the actions and promises of others; honour has always to me appeared so dear to French officers.

I always cherish the esteem of good citizens. If there exist at St. Domingo any ambitious men, who covet nothing but honour, preferment, or distinction; as for me, my ambition always consisted in meriting the honourable consideration of good men, in seeing my fellow citizens happy; in enjoying, in common with them, the sole title of free man, the sole rights of equality, in the bosom of my tranquil family, and in the circle of a few estimable friends.

You advise, my dear Comrade, to pay no regard to my outlawry; General Leclerc, you tell me, has said it should not have taken place had he known me sooner, and that the Proclamation should be an-nulled as soon as I should have retracted my error. I am ready to retract, but my doubts must be removed, my suspicions cleared up. There is no sacrifice that I will not make for the peace and happiness of my fellow citizens, if I am but convinced that they shall all be free and happy. I have but one thing left to sacrifice—my life, all the rest I have already made. Produce the proofs necessary for my conviction, and with a willing heart I offer the sacrifice, if, after demonstration of my error, it can make atonement, and restore tranquillity and prosperity to my country, and to my fellow citizens.

I salute you with friendship.

(Signed)   H. Christophe.

Nº XIII.

Petite Anse, 30th Germinal, year 10.

Vilton, Commandant at La Petite Anse, to Citizen Henry Christophe, General of Brigade, commanding the Cordon of the North.

MY DEAR COMRADE,

I CAN with difficulty express the pleasure that your answer to my letter affords me, since it gives me the hope of seeing you once more actuated by that confidence which you should never have ceased to place in the justice and generosity of the representative of France in this colony; these are the general characteristics of French officers, and, above all, of the general in chief, Leclerc; and it was

the intimate knowledge of these qualities,
that induced the First Consul to make
choice of him as the bearer of happiness
and peace to this unfortunate colony.
Your submission to a chief of such merit
will gain you a protector, who will charge
himself with the office of making such
provision for you as will lead you to bless
the day of your compliance with the
counsel I have given, and which I now
repeat more strongly than ever. I made it
my first business to communicate your letter to him, as well as to General Hardy.
The expressions you make use of have met
with their approbation. The distrust you
discover in some paragraphs alone pre-
vents them from being completely satisfied.
The general in chief himself is going to
write to you. I cannot press you too
strongly to place entire confidence in his
promises, as well as in the honour of
General Hardy; and I doubt not but you
will find in their letters every thing that

you, as well as your fellow citizens, ought, in reason, to require for your satisfaction.

With respect to your friend Granier, if he is detained, it is not because of his connections, but because he has many enemies here, who have calumniated him. I have no doubt, that, as soon as Government shall have had leisure to investigate his affair, he will be immediately set at liberty.

Adieu, my dear Comrade: depend upon the friendship I have sworn to you for life.

Health and friendship.

(Signed)   VILTON.

N° XIV.

Head Quarters, Robillard, Grand Boucan,
2d Floreal, Year 10.

The General of Brigade, Henry Christophe,
commanding the Cordon of the North, to
Vilton, Commandant at La Petit Anse.

I AGAIN receive, with pleasure, in your
letter of the 30th ultimo, the expression
of your friendship for me. The successful issue of your correspondence, which
you seem to hope, depends upon General
Leclerc. He has, indeed, addressed to me
a letter ; but I have read in it, with dis-
gust, the proposition it contains, of dis-
honouring myself by an act of monstrous
cowardice and perfidy.

I do trust, however, that in the character
which has been given him of me, if dictated
by truth, it has not been represented, that

such actions were familiar to me, and that
I was wholly divested of every sentiment
of delicacy and honour.

I replied to his letter in the same
manner as I did to that addressed to me
by General Hardy, which appeared to be
written in that style of frankness which
ought to distinguish a soldier.

I have every desire to abjure the distrust which I have conceived. I demand
of those two Generals no more than what
is necessary to renounce it ; that is, in
fact, the code of laws which was promised
us by the proclamation addressed to us by
the consuls of the republic, when they
communicated the constitution of year 8.
In such a code only can lie the proof of
the intention to maintain and consolidate
liberty and equality. If these laws are in
your possession, impart them to me; if
they exist, and you have them not, endeavour to obtain and produce them to me.
To them I look for the restoration of tran-

quillity to this country, for the cement of
union between the French of both worlds,
for a stop to the effusion of their blood,
for the reconciliation with the republic of
her children, who never willingly renounced her; and for the re-establishment,
in this island, of peace and its blessings,
in lieu of civil war and its ravages. Openly
proclaim this code, and let the light of
truth shine on those who may be blinded
with error; then will you enjoy the satisfaction of having contributed to the happiness of our country, to that of our fellow
citizens, to my own amongst the rest; for,
whatever lot may await me, my happiness
will consist in that of my brethren, were
it even sealed with my blood.

The unfortunate Granier is detained,
and, without doubt, you tell me, on account of some calumnious insinuations of
his enemies. Ought such a detention to
have taken place without evidence? and
is it consistent with a just and impartial

government to suffer such long delays in the production of the proofs requisite for just condemnation, or equitable acquittal? But, placed as I am, does it become me to plead the cause of friendship?

My dear comrade, do not forget these laws about which I have been speaking to you. Communicate them to me without delay, and you will soon attain the object you seem to aim at in your correspondence.

I salute you in friendship.

(Signed)   HENRY CHRISTOPHE.

A true copy of the originals deposited in the archives of the state,

Compte de LIMONADE,

Secretary of State, Minister of Foreign Affairs.

At Cape Henry, by P. Roux,
Printer to the King.

NARRATIVE

OF THE

ACCESSION OF THEIR ROYAL MAJESTIES

TO THE

THRONE OF HAYTI,

BEFORE entering upon the narrative of the accession of their Royal Majesties to the throne, we deem it our duty to lay before our readers a succinct exposition of the principal events which have occurred, and of the principal operations antecedent to this happy day of everlasting memory.

The Haytian people had scarcely breathed, after their deliverance from the presence of those Vandals who have ravaged every country into which their well-known footsteps have strayed, and just freed from disorders, a brigand-like spirit, and from anarchy, when our inde-dependence began to be established, the state became organized—commerce, agriculture, and navigation flourished—our internal fortifications were completed;— at length the Haytians, reunited, reconciled, perceived that there existed and could exist for them no other country in the globe than these happy and fortunate climes, which the sun delights to illumine, abundantly pouring forth, with a complacent heat, all the benignity of his beneficent rays on the fields in which are to be found, in unparalleled plenty, those fruits of delicious flavour, and those trees loaded with the precious aromatic juices of Arabia, which produce the real nectar so much esteemed and so generally prized, its cottons, cacaos, &c. and so many other productions with which bounteous Nature hath endowed Hayti, in the measure of its goodness, the true attribute of Divine Providence; when our happiness was all at once totally and utterly subverted. Insubordination and licentiousness found their way into our armies; some perfidious men, who sold themselves to the enemy, organized a conspiracy, of which history furnishes but few examples; and in the sequel, Dessalines, the chief of the government, was assassinated. The public treasures were squandered, a few of the conspirators seized the spoils of the unfortunate state, dark and secret plots were agitated in the different regiments, calumny pointed its shafts, and intrigue was busy. The Haytians took up arms, and all the evils that were sought and fomented by the enemies of Hayti, speedily became realized to afflict anew these beautiful countries. Henry foresaw all that was accumulating to oppress his native land; he saw that the storm was particularly di-

rected against the heads of the illustrious
and incorruptible defenders of liberty ;
and that, this being accomplished, the factions proposed to themselves nothing less
than to substitute themselves in their place,
to deliver over the country to our enemies,
to fascinate and lull the multitude by promises and presents of pretended promotion, which were offered with a too culpable facility, in order to effect the more
certain attainment of their criminal
ends.

Great at all times—ever the same—and
reared and brought up in revolutions—in
the midst of the din of arms, he was un-
moved at this;—he knew what the traitors
and other loose characters, who had given
rise to the evils of a civil war, were capable of. His energy and his resolution
augmented with the dangers which he had
to overcome; he braved the fury of the
storm, put forth all his efforts, and shewed
himself, with the rapidity of lightning,

wherever his presence was required ; he dispersed and punished the traitors, revived the courage of the brave, and succeeded in triumphing over the efforts of the wicked.

On the 18th of December 1806, in a proclamation dated from the citadel Henry, he points out the secret agents of those ambitious men who had made themselves busy, in every way, in corrupting the troops.

The 24th, he proceeded to disperse the collection of troublesome spirits assembled at Port aux Crimes, who were holding a consultation under arms, yet reeking with the blood of those martyrs to liberty whom they had sacrificed to their rage, their ambition, and cupidity.

The 1st of January 1807, he fought the famous battle of Cibert, routing and cutting in pieces the army of Petion, who was himself obliged to throw away his decorations, in order to protect his flight, and then plunged into a morass up to his neck, before returning to Port aux Crimes.

Henry then lays siege to this rebel city, but reflecting upon the number of conspirators whom he had left in the rear, added to those who abounded in the army, and whose inflammatory expressions were scarcely concealed ; and considering the horrors that must ensue from the capture of a city by assault, he postponed the conquest of it, and marched his troops back to their cantonments.

A council of state, composed of the generals and eminent citizens, who saw the necessity of establishing in these tempestuous times an order of things, was speedily convoked, and they instituted the constitution of the 17th of February 1807, which decreed to the chief magistrate the title of President of Hayti.

The 19th of February, he offered, through the medium of a proclamation distinguished for its good sense, a general amnesty, and oblivion of the past to all the revolted.

Without being diverted from the great conceptions he had formed, he organizes the civil and commercial tribunals; nominates to vacant places in the army, as well as in the magistracy; stimulates the work of cultivation by the establishment of companies of agriculturists, known by the name of " Police Guards," composed of managers and heads of houses, the utility of which is now so generally admitted, both on account of the public security and the improvement of cultivation; he moreover restored public instruction in full activity, examined into the administration of the public hospitals, and carried into every branch of the service that penetrating eye which embraces all the details, without their detracting fom the vast conception of the whole.

The insurrection continued to spread, and the Haytians, not knowing what they really wanted, urged by that restless spirit which seems natural to them, take up arms and stir up a revolt, stimulated by harangues from the rebellious. The most beneficial acts of the government; the regularly established pay of the troops ; the buying up of the coffee, that judicious measure, so well calculated to enhance the value of our territorial commodities; all became, in the mouths of these infuriate demagogues, so many pretexts for an insurrection of the troops, as well as of that important though unenlightened body of the people, the cultivators. The good deeds of the government thus became as instruments in the hands of calumniators, with which they had the audacity to combat it. One issue of specie, from the public treasury, of 227 thousand gourd bottles, for the purpose of accomplishing that very laudable object of paying for coffee at 20 *sous* to the growers, ought of itself to prove, to men of good faith, at once the greatness of the plan, the advantages that must result from it, and the solicitude of the government that ordained it.

In the beginning of June 1807, from the extremity of the insurrection of the Moustiques the president repairs in haste before the town of the Gonaïves, which was sold to the rebels by treason, and in a few days he compelled them to reimbark with disgrace, whilst the greater part of the revolted, after having got possession of Arcahaye, presented themselves before St. Marc; yet, when informed of the arrival of the President and of the flight of Bazelais, the rebels did not think proper to wait for him, but withdrew themselves into their Port aux Crimes; they were pursued on their way, without a possibility of being overtaken, so precipitate was their flight!

In July, some troops under the command of Lamarre were sent against the insurgents of Port de Paix. The ninth corps rose in a mass, and deserted the cause of legitimate authority. The President marched, and on the other side of the mountains of St. Louis repulsed the rebels, pursued them from post to post up to the very forts of Port de Paix, where they intrenched themselves. He there attacked them in order, displaying the rare endowments of his energy and courage, and concluded, in less than fifteen days, a memorable campaign, which was followed by the dispersion of Lamarre, the capture of all the forts at Port de Paix, and a great number of prisoners.

A complaint, brought on by the fatigues of this campaign, suspended his complete reduction of the rebels. The operations were not followed up with vigour; they contented themselves with keeping possession of the town of Port de Paix, and with too much confidence despised or neglected pursuing a small body of the fugitives who were still in the

woods. A fatal error! strong reinforce-
ments were sent to Lamarre; the rebels,
by the help of their barges discovered a
method of maintaining their accomplices
and furnishing them with ammunition.
Lamarre, on this, rallies his partisans and
makes his appearance at Damalo, an advantageous position in the mountains,
distant some leagues from Port de Paix.

The President, scarcely recovered from
his indisposition, and yet in a state of con-
valescence, sets out to place himself at the
head of the troops; he again dislodges
the revolted from all the positions they occupied, and charges them himself at the
head of his staff; they broke and fled, pursued on all sides. Henry now saw, with
emotion, that these unhappy men were
undeceived, and about to renounce their
errors.

During this expedition the troops of the
west rivalled those of the north in valour
and achievements, in again subduing the

revolted who had the audacity to **attack** the line. It was on the memorable 20th of September, when eight battalions of faithful troops got the better of twenty-one of the revolted, who were intrenched and in the most advantageous position. This instance is a proof that bravery is inseparable from honour and fidelity. These rebel troops who could not bear the sight and presence of those under the legitimate authority, are nevertheless the same who conquered the south under the French armies.

Whilst the rebellion seemed to acquire consistency in the south, the legitimate authority found one of its firmest defenders in General Jean Baptiste Perrier, called Gauman, who separated from the revolters, erected the standard of fidelity and honour in the mountains of the great Bay of Jeremy; rallied his brethren, enlightened them ; undeceived them respecting the absurd calumnies of the revolters, and paid homage to the President, whom he acknowledges as the only chief to whom he wished and ought to pay obedience. His successes, aided by the means that were dispatched to him, brought about a useful and fortunate diversion: he kept the rebels constantly in check and in perpetual alarm : he pounced, with the rapidity of the eagle, upon the places where he was not expected, leaving behind him traces of his having been there, and retired into inaccessible fastnesses, which he knew how to select, from the moment that a superior force marched against him: he showed himself too incorruptible by any of the caresses and promises which the revolters had tendered, to attract him to their cause : he braved at once their menaces and their stratagems, and shewed himself always unconquerable.

Such brilliant expeditions as these we have enumerated, not having yet sickened the revolters, so blind is presump-

tion! they again directed, towards the
end of October, an attempt against St.
Marc. The President repaired to this
town, and the day after his arrival caused
them to be attacked at the habitations
Pivert and Florenceau, where they had
gained time sufficient to intrench themselves head high. The day of the 25th
was rendered doubly memorable by the
two actions which took place, at the termination of which the rebels were overthrown and pursued with desperate vigour
by the horse guards of the President. A
great number of prisoners was made, and
the fields of battle were covered with dead
bodies. The chests and colours of the
rebel army fell into our possession. Then
were to be seen the miseries of war displayed in all their horror; wretched fugitives wandering about, lost in the woods,
perishing of hunger and of thirst, venting
imprecations against those traitors who
had exposed them to so deplorable a lot,

and running, like new Europeans, to
the sea-shore in the hope of regaining
their vessels which were kept at anchor, as
the only refuge in which they could find
safety. It was on this day too that the
brilliant valour of our troops was so con-
spicuous ; but particular praise is here due
to the 2d and 3d battalions of the 2d
regiment, and the 1st battalion of the 27th,
which after a fatiguing march of thirty-six
leagues without resting, contributed so
effectually to the glory of this day. The
women of St. Marc have afforded on this,
as well as on preceding and subsequent
occasions, proofs of patriotism and ardent
devotion to their country's cause, such as
characterised the ancient Spartans. Spec-
tators of the combat, they applauded from
the top of the ramparts the valour of our
troops, and were the first to shout aloud
the cry of victory. Their generous cares
have brought alleviation and comfort to
the aid of suffering humanity, by their

affording in the most ample manner that relief to the wounded which their state demanded.

Gratitude has since rewarded the zeal and fidelity of the province of the West, with the appellation bestowed upon St. Marc, *of the faithful,* a title equally honourable and glorious to her.

The enemy being driven away, the President, with his accustomed activity, set out from St. Marc the 28th, and on the 1st of November he was at Port de Paix, after having passed the Great Hill, and traversed the mountains of St. Louis ; without resting, he marched over those of Port de Paix, caused the rebels to evacuate the formidable position of Calvary, which they had got possession of, then returned to the city of Port de Paix, organised a system of attack as well of defence, and on the 7th he returned to his capital.

In the course of September in the year following, the revolters not being yet sickened by their repeated defeats, were to receive a new proof of the inutility of their endeavours. One of their most formidable expeditions from the Port aux Crimes, to compose which they had put in requisition every body from infancy to old age, menaced the *cordon* of the west at all points, whilst Lamarre, by a bold stroke, takes post, with all the forces that he could collect in the centre of the mountains of Port de Paix, menacing the city at the same time.

In the west, the camps of Colleau, Lacroix, Dubourg, and the post of Verrier, were successively attacked, and became the theatre of the valour of our troops, and that of the losses of the enemy. The insurgents in the mean time send out detachments to pillage and set on fire all solitary and unprotected houses, a species of brigand-like warfare in which they excel; then reuniting their troops, they form the project of laying siege to St.

Marc, but at a very respectful distance;
they take up a position at Langeae Ros-
sineau, Jeanton, and Charette; there, thinking themselves secure, they organize camps;
no longer confiding in their numbers, they
raise intrenchment upon intrenchment, of
double and triple stages, and construct
gigantic works, hastening all the while the
receipt of ammunition and provisions supplied by means of their corsairs, which
they keep at anchor in the Bay of La-
conde.

In this position they remained for
twenty-five days; but hunger began to be
felt, and considerable detachments from
the main body traversed the mountains to
maraud for provisions, but the moveable
columns of our army repulsed them at the
point of the bayonet every time they appeared before the plantations.

The operation next commenced was
the attack of the rebels at Charette, who,
by means of our well served batteries, sus-

tained a considerable loss, which had the effect of obliging them to dig trenches to afford them shelter from our bombs and bullets, which were directed to intercept their procuring water and every kind of provisions.

It was determined to occupy the position of Mary, in the rear of the enemy, so as to cut off their retreat. I know that our intrepid general thought of nothing less than requesting to have the disposal of a part of the forces of the west, to pass by the mountains, and possess himself of the city of Port aux Crimes, destitute as it was of troops, while the rebels were dying of hunger, hemmed in around all their positions.

In the mean time the squadron with stores and provisions, which had left the Cape to go to the relief of St. Marc, did arrive; calm winds had detained it on its passage, but with what pleasure was it descried by our army in full sail after the rebel barks, and in the act of capturing seven of their corsairs that were leaving the Port aux Crimes with ammunition and necessaries, which they were carrying to the relief of their accomplices; the rest saved themselves by superior sailing. Our operations were then carried on with more activity, and it was determined that new and vigorous measures should be adopted for defeating the insurgents, and allowing them no time to breathe. Positions were taken up within pistol shot; and the insurgents, closely cooped up, cannonaded or killed off, no more dared to make their appearance; so that every outlet being guarded to cut off their retreat, we in a great measure calculated upon their being reduced; but on the 18th of November the rebels made their escape by a road abandoned ever since the revolution, and covered with shrubs and logwood, which had been deemed impracticable; they were, nevertheless, pursued,

and it is said, that in this affair Petion
disguised himself in female attire, many
women being about the camp, and that
thus our troops allowed him to pass on,
intent only on pursuing men with arms
in their hands. The places abandoned
by the rebels presented the appearance in
reality of a churchyard, in consequence
of the great number of graves they con-
tained.

Lamarre having, as we already observed, taken up his position in the mountains of Port de Paix, and fortified it in
an equal degree with that of Port aux
Crimes, saw himself surrounded in a similar manner, and in want of every thing;
he burnt with the rage of despair, made
attack upon attack, which being uni-
formly repulsed, compelled him to retire
into his intrenchments, not without considerable loss. To furnish some idea of
the fury displayed in this quarter, a fury
only to be found in civil wars, the most

formidable ramparts on both sides, were
built up, one against another, so that no
one could venture to lift up his head
without being immediately shot. Extreme
and indeed frightful means were employed
to annihilate these madmen ; subterranean
engagements took place; sappers and
miners would work with indefatigable
perseverance to blow up the fortifications
of each other, and whole battalions of
grenadiers were sent into the air ; the
ground covered with mangled limbs, the
dying and the dead, while others found
their grave in the bowels of the earth.
What a distressing picture for humanity !
let us however pursue it, for truth requires
I should not disguise our sufferings.
Those same ramparts, when destroyed,
were as soon occupied again : a murderous
fire was kept up from the ruins, whilst new
ramparts were erecting to replace the first.
At length, after a thousand engagements,
famine, losses, disease, and desertions,

compelled the insurgents to break through the lines and retire into the Mole!

The quarters of Gros-Morne, the mountains of Port de Paix, of Monstigne, and of Jean Rabel, then breathed once more; the cultivators returned to their labours, the army formed a cordon in the mountains which surround the Mole, and besieged that place.

In the Spanish part, some conspirators sold to the insurgents, such as Stephen Albert and Gilbert, endeavoured to deceive them in exciting them against us, but they received the reward of their treason at their own hands.

The skilful policy of the President took advantage of the happy moment of the usurpation of the Spanish monarchy in Europe to draw closer the ties of amity with those in Hayti. He had long conceived that, as inhabitants of the same soil, a similarity of wants ought to unite us with our brethren, the Spanish Haytians, when the same enemies menace our existence. To this effect, he sounds their inclinations; he finds them equally well disposed with his own ; he dispatches arms and warlike stores to the general, Don Juan Sanchez Ramirez, and by these generous aids he enables him to undertake offensive operations against the city of St. Domingo, to attack the place whither Ferrand had taken refuge with the French troops who still occupied this point, and finally to expel them from it.

He restores the ancient ties of friendship and of trade with this just, loyal, and sensible people, and the result has proved that he has had no occasion to repent of it.

The fury of contention which we have thus slightly sketched, did not however prevent the chief of the government from directing his attention, even amid camps, to the welfare of the people. He had perceived that a wise administration of the revenues of the state could alone save it.

Men of unimpeachable integrity replaced those who did not stand so clear in their office. A commission for the examination of the public accounts was established ; the state then began to feel the immensity of its resources ; the troops were clothed, equipped, and paid ; a navy was all at once created, and our seamen already, who had only been accustomed to manœuvre in slight vessels, learnt, with the aid of the compass, how to navigate ships of three masts, to cruise in the most stormy latitudes, and to surmount the fury of the storms. The Haytian flag displayed itself on the astonished ocean, and with surprise and admiration was seen a new people in the history of navigation.

Not only did this navy become the terror of the insurgents, but it wrested from them the empire of the seas, of which they had become so vain.

The citadel Henry, that palladium of liberty, that majestic bulwark of inde-

pendence, that monument of the greatness
and of the vast combinations of a Henry,
is built on the lofty summit of one of the
highest mountains in the island, whence
you may discover, to the left, the island
of Tortuga, and the reflection of its beautiful canal ; in front, the gentle risings,
with the city of Cape Henry, its roadstead,
and the vast expanse of the ocean. On
the right, La Grange, Monte Christ, the
city of Fort Royal, Mancheneel Bay, and
the surrounding hills. The eye is gratified
with the prospect of the beautiful plain,
and the magnificent carpet of verdure
spread before it.

At the back, the extended chain of
mountains seems, as it were, the frame to
this enchanting picture. The position,
fortified by nature, and to which art has
added all its science, with casemates and
bomb proofs, has secured it from being
successfully besieged, while the mouths of
the cannon overtop the elevation of the

high ground, and command the adjacent
territory, affording protection to the whole
of the north, and indeed of Hayti itself,
this being the most formidable defence it
possesses.

The fortifications in the interior, if
they had but the sole advantage of having
taught us to regard lightly the capture of
our sea-ports, would always claim a great
degree of importance in that point of view
alone. A nation impressed with the conviction that the guarantee of individual
protection to its members, exists only in
favoured situations of ground, and that
this guarantee is to be found only in its
valour, in the sacrifices it is willing to un-
dergo, and moreover, in the woods and
mountains that are familiar to its inhabitants ;—such a nation, I say, will not de-
spond at the temporary abandonment of
some villages, which good policy and salutary precaution may have induced them
to set on fire at the approach of its ene-

G

mies; particularly when, on a proper foresight, it is actually necessary, in order to baffle the designs of their oppressors, providing themselves, at the same time, with every thing necessary, to resist all such attacks as may be directed against them.

Sans Souci, a town rising into preference, and likely to become the capital of Hayti, has been established. Ravines have been filled up, mountains levelled, and public roads laid out. This superb royal palace, the glory of Hayti, is carried up to a great elevation; the beauty and durability of its construction, its sumptuous apartments, all with inlaid work, and lined with the most beautiful and rarest tapestry, which was amassed at a great expense, and with particular care in the selection.

The furniture, and elegant tapestry, are selected with good taste, the gardens arranged with a just symmetry, through which meanders a pure stream, having a degree of freshness that particularly characterizes it, the jets d'eau, the fruit trees, and European productions, &c. &c. combine to embellish the retreat of a hero, and to attract the admiration of strangers; whilst a church, whose noble dome agreeably points out the richness of its architecture, and other public establishments, such as arsenals, dock-yards, and barracks, have sprung up around in spite of the ravages of war. To see the astonishing activity diffused in all these works, one would say that the greatest tranquillity had prevailed, and that it was the hand of peace which brought them to perfection ; immense treasures, the fruits of economy in the public administration of finances, fill the spacious coffers of the citadel Henry.

I know it to be one of the intentions of our King to have the rotunda of his palace in the citadel paved and lined with quadruples. He is rich enough to do this.

Such a novel species of apartment will reflect a precious drapery, and be without parallel in the world. On the frontispiece of this monument the motto of Louis XIV should be inscribed,

Nec pluribus impar.

A worthy minister of religion, and philanthropic author, the Abbé Gregoire, who, since the commencement of his career, has devoted his pen to the investigation of truth, and the defence of humanity, has, by his affecting work on the Literature of the Negroes, written with all the eloquence and simplicity of truth, avenged our rights by openly publishing. in the face of his countrymen, at once their crimes and the injustice of the pretended superiority of their species over ours. The President read his work with all that interest it inspires, and has voted him his thanks conveyed in a Haytian work called " The Cry of Nature," which do equal honour to the virtuous prelate to whom they are addressed, and the head of the government conferring such a mark of respect, at once public and flattering in its acknowledgment.

The siege of the Mole was converted into a blockade by sea and land: the President was desirous of reducing the rebels and sparing the effusion of blood at the same time. It was in their cruise before this place that our seamen served their apprenticeship, and attained that superiority which has since distinguished them. One trait of these John Barts of the new world ought not to be passed over in silence. The Foudroyant having missed the anchorage at the platform early in the night of the 28th of March, 1809, drifted into the midst of five vessels of the rebel party, who were endeavouring secretly to throw succours into the Cape. The captain of this ship kept them all in check by

a bold manœuvre, and the fire of mus-
quetry and great guns until daylight, when
our squadron was enabled to go to his
assistance and extricate him, pursuing the
rebels to their hiding places, after having
frustrated the object of their expedition.

Four months after this event a new in-
cursion took place, after the manner of
that of September, 1808; having again
for its object to bring off Lamarre. The
rebels had forgotten the many defeats they
had experienced in so many quarters, they
wanted one lesson more, which they
speedily received; but being too well acquainted with the environs of St. Marc,
they contented themselves with appearing
before the Mirebalais, and when they were
about to be attacked, nearly the whole of
their forces retreated a great way into the
Spanish part, and then fell unexpectedly
upon the spring and the great river, having
promised themselves nothing less, in the

height of folly and presumption, than a march upon the Capital, as they had pompously given out.

The President, informed of the projects of the rebels, would not take any step to give them a confidence which he was sure they would abuse: the event has justified his conjectures. It was only on their arrival in front of the spring, that troops were sent against them to harass them. Without giving the rebels time to recollect themselves, they were immediately attacked and routed. The perfidious David Trois, commandant of the expedition, lost his life on the occasion; many of their noted chiefs fell into our power, pursued by our troops, who effected a junction with those of the west, in the Spanish Savannas: on their arrival at Banique, they found the l'Artibonite swollen with rain. One party attempted to cross it by swimming, and were carried away by the flood. Our army being close up, the attack became extremely animated; the horse guards of the President charged, cutting down or dispersing in every direction all opposed to them. The loss of men drowned is estimated at two battalions. Lamarre attempted also to make an attack upon our cordon of troops; but he found a wall of brass which he could never pierce, and abandoned his enterprise, his horse, two aid-de-camps, and a multitude of his accomplices on the field.

The following paragraph contains a very just and sensible reflection, extracted from the general orders to the army of 17th of August, 1809, which give a narrative of these two victories.

" It is in vain that the mild policy of his Serene Highness the Lord President induces him to abstain from attacking the revolted, in order to afford them time for repentance. These ungrateful beings are unmindful of his paternal intentions; they falsely imagine, because he does not carry

fire and sword into their dwellings, when
the innocent would fall victims to such a
disaster, that there are no means of reducing them; but the most efficacious
method of reducing them is to leave them
to themselves. In their intense blindness
they come to receive the punishment due
to their crimes."

The disorganized faction that had
placed Petion at its head, seeing he did
not accord with their wishes to the end
they proposed to themselves, and otherwise
convinced by their experience of his want
of talents and of energy, solicited the recall of Rigaud, a man who was born evidently for the ill luck of his country, when
we consider the sad and deplorable effects
produced by his rebellion against the Governor Louverture, misfortunes which are
but too well known. To conceal their
projects, and the end which the perfidious
government that employs him proposes to
itself, and to gull and deceive respecting

his connivance, they caused him to adopt
the pretext of an escape, as if nothing could
be more easy than to lull the vigilance of
a restless and suspicious police, such as
that established by Bonaparte in his states,
whose spies and agents abound in every
court, and likewise in all parts of the
globe, to carry into effect the plans of
their master. One must be blind indeed
to suppose that a hapless islander (especially of his colour) could be able to save
himself from the dungeons in which he
had pined, so long as the occasion did not
offer of administering to the purposes expected of him. Besides, his arrival, and
the means by which he set about it, were
sufficient to do away with all doubt in
that respect. He sets out then under a
feigned and disguised name; he is accompanied by two aides-de-camp, which leads
to an evident supposition of the part they
intend he should act. He reaches the
United States, directed and recommended

to some French agents. He keeps himself concealed, not to excite suspicion, and to shun an exposure. Notwithstanding, he is marked out by the friends of our government; he slips away and avoids the British cruisers, and on the 7th April 1810, towards night, arrives at Aux Cayes. He is received with welcome by those of his partisans whose foolish and presumptuous hopes he had excited; but the majority of good citizens conceal themselves or remain silent; they do not allow themselves to be stunned by the declamations of this pretended martyr to liberty, this contemptible apostle of falsehood, this sneaking instrument of our enemies, who comes to aid their criminal endeavours. He soon repairs to Port aux Crimes; having been unsuccessful in recovering the tatters of this usurped authority, for the traitors do not agree amongst themselves, he returns to Aux Cayes with the most crafty of his partisans, and there he at length concludes by bringing about a division between the department of the south and that portion of the west occupied by the rebels, till he may at length substitute himself in the room of Petion, the present object of his ambition.

Hence springs a most sorrowful consideration for humanity. We know that our dissensions give joy to the friends of slavery, that our common tyrants wish to see them during all our days, and that they calculate upon nothing short of a total annihilation of the population of Hayti, whom they wish to replace by new wretches transplanted from the regions of Africa. We are thoroughly acquainted with the whole extent of their villainy; and we seem eager, in our rivalry, to serve them effectually, by carrying on the work of destruction amongst ourselves. O delirium of the passions! O inconceivable fatality! to what lengths will men suffer themselves to be carried who listen to the

false illusions of ambition! May we not
apprehend that our enemies will, with
justice, apply to us these two verses?

> Too prodigal of blood, they ought to stay,
> As our avengers, they each other slay.

Rigaud is the more culpable, that, after
having experienced at different times the
effects of the wiles of the French government, he still consents, a third time, to become again their tool, and to labour for the
destruction of his fellow-countrymen. Enlightened as he is, the language he ought
to have held, when he touched the soil of
Hayti, would have been at once becoming
and easily expressed.

" I return," he should have said to the
head of the government, " from that barbarous country, where, as the reward of
my easy compliance, I was left to languish
in dungeons; I have heard deliberations
on the ruin of my fellow-citizens. Wel-
comed from the moment when they thought

I might cooperate in this abominable design, I found myself afterwards treated
and caressed; they put my ambition to
the test; they offered me a fortune and the
restoration of the former rank I held.
But, senseless men! how could they think
that I was so devoid of reason and of good
sense, so easy and so stupid as to lend myself to their criminal designs? The two cruel
lessons of experience I have undergone
have instructed me too well. I have dis-
sembled, I have consented to all; I have
promised every thing to extricate myself
from the fetters of bondage. My first
thought, on reaching this classic land of
liberty, is that of acknowledging the reign-
ing sovereign, whose cause is inseparable
from mine. To him I owe the confession
of former errors, and at his feet I ought to
lay my repentance. I swear fidelity to
him, and henceforth to labour in consolidating the liberty and independence of
my country, the sole end for which I took

up arms." Truly, and we do not hesitate
to say, had he maintained such language
as this, had he employed his influence in
reclaiming Petion and his associates to
right principles, had he not sought to dis-
member the state that he might appro-
priate to himself its spoils, he would have
been received with open arms by the head
of the government, who would have par-
doned his faults, and overlooked his past
errors, as he would have wished that God
might pardon them; and finally, he would
have drawn down upon him the blessings
of the people; instead of which, by pursuing a line of conduct diametrically opposite, he has prepared for himself the most
inauspicious omens, and, as a final prospect, he digs his own grave and that of
his partisans.

" You have been the first" (said the
head of the government to Bonnet, when
after the decease of the Emperor he came
to the Cape) " to exhibit to the troops

breaches of discipline, so that when you wished to restore order and duty amongst them, you could never effect it ; they will turn their arms against you, yourselves, when once tainted with crime. To prolong your existence, you will be obliged to allow them to do whatever they please. When the treasures of the state which you have dilapidated, shall become exhausted, you can no longer pay them ; you will be constrained to have recourse to extreme measures, and to suffer the fatal effects of all their licentiousness. As for Petion, I pity him ; instead of being the chief, he is only the slave and instrument of your faction. When he shall be well drawn in, and on affairs becoming desperate, you will abandon him, as you, Bonnet, particularly, did with General Vilatte, whose ruin you were the cause of on the 30th Ventose. In exciting a civil war, you will be responsible for all the mischiefs that will be the result of it, for one knows very

well the day when the sword is drawn
from the scabbard, but no one can tell
when it shall be put up again."

What words could be more prophetic
than these? All that Henry had predicted
has come to pass. The chief instigator of
the most signal treason has seen himself,
in his turn, betrayed, abandoned by the
perfidious wretches who had drawn him
into the abyss. Has not Bonnet been one
of the first to go and join Rigaud, and to
declare himself against the rebel Petion?

To resume the thread of the narrative.
The President having employed all the
means which his great mind could devise,
and despairing of getting possession of the
Mole unless by force of arms, resolved to
take the command in person of the troops
who were besieging it; and after vigorous
operations, in which he displayed his talents in the great art of war, he had the
glory of making himself master of this
famous rebel city, and of causing those

H

who defended it to lay down their arms at discretion, after the two principal leaders had lost their lives in the place.

The operations alone of this siege would require a very lengthened work to describe, for they abound in traits of bravery and heroism which belong to the Haytian nation.

Subjoined is the Proclamation which the President addressed to the army after the taking of this city, and which so well paints the sentiments of his heart.

State of Hayti.

PROCLAMATION.

HENRY CHRISTOPHE,

*President and Generalissimo of the Land and
Sea Forces,*

TO THE LAND AND NAVAL ARMAMENTS OF THE
STATE OF HAYTI.

SOLDIERS!

THE place of St. Nicholas Mole has just fallen by the success of your arms, rebellion is extinguished in this quarter, and you have planted on every side the colours of the legitimate authority, already so distinguished by the numerous triumphs obtained over the enemies of liberty.

Twenty days of regular siege have sufficed to destroy, to the very foundations, those fortresses which parricidal hands had raised in defence of rebellion. In vain a pretending expedition had flattered itself with the hope of perpetuating intestine dissensions, and sacrificing at the shrine of error; your arms, strengthened by the most just of causes, have, in a few days, overthrown these edifices, and buried under their ruins the projects and presumptive hopes of a criminal faction.

Weary of temporising measures, that had for their object to spare the effusion of blood, and having perceived that nothing could equal my patience and my kindness, but the obduracy and the inflexibility of the factious, I decided on the fate of this guilty place. The two chiefs, who successively took the command of it, have bitten the dust; two of their vessels of war being shattered, presented in the roads nothing more than unavailing skeletons; a considerable pile of

cannon, of mortars, of stores, and provisions of every kind, are the results of
your toils, and the reward of your valour ;
while these men, who have issued from
the extremity of the south, with the intent
to deprive you of the most precious of all
blessings, now obliged to surrender at discretion, have experienced that your clemency is equal to your valour.

Such is ever the recompence of true
courage! Nothing can resist it, because
it is maintained by fidelity to one's chief,
guided by honour, and inspired by patriotism.—Soldiers, and you, brave seamen,
who have rivalled in all respects the land
forces, you whose efforts have braved the
winds, the currents, and the waves, in a
cruise which will be the admiration of all
who are experienced in naval affairs, the
new lustre which your glorious exploits
have just reflected upon the arms of your
chief is your best eulogium. In truth, the
zeal, the constancy, the loyalty, the fide-

lity, and the intrepidity which you have displayed in a multitude of engagements, which were rendered necessary through the most inconceivable animosity, constitute at once my glory and my pride ; yes, I have found in you the most intrepid warriors, who have contributed to the establishment of liberty and independence, and I have, more than once, in this campaign, gloried in being at your head. It is indeed gratifying to me to declare solemnly, that you have all deserved well of the country ! and that it will be a satisfaction for my heart to decree honorary rewards to those of you who have most distinguished themselves.

But to acquire distinction in the career of heroes is not all ; there is another virtue, another species of glory of which we ought to furnish an example.

You have seen the inveterate supporters of error, the obstinate partisans of a cause revolting to reason as well as to nature ; you have seen them, I say, these unhappy children of the south, basely abandoned and betrayed by their comrades, after having experienced all that human misfortunes have in them of extremest bitterness, after having been compelled to lay down their arms, to come and throw themselves at my feet, to acknowledge their errors, and implore my clemency ; they thought to find in me an irritated conqueror ; they expected to read in my offended front their sentence to die. Ungrateful men ! they have only been witnesses of my compassion, and of the tears which their repentance has wrung from me. You too, soldiers, melted at this example, have nobly shared with them your tents, you clothing, and your food ; they have found no other than brethren in you, and your arms have carefully borne their sick and wounded to the hospitals, to be treated and attended in the same manner as your

own companions. But still more, the 9th
regiment, that same one which first raised
the standard of revolt, as well as the remains of the 16th, 18th, 21st, 22d, 23d,
and 24th, made prisoners, are to-day astonished at taking rank in the army of
Hayti; but let their astonishment cease
when they know that in punishing, a father is always paternal; and let them re-
member these words of the common Father of mankind: " There is more joy in
heaven over that one sheep which is found
again, than for the whole flock that hath
never strayed."

May this trait of magnanimity soften
the hearts of those who still foment or encourage calumny! Let them at length
understand that it is good to sacrifice private passions to the general benefit; let
them consider that the vile agents of the
French government, like greedy vultures,
are only watching an opportunity to fall
upon their prey; let them reflect, that the

vessel of independence in which we are all embarked, must save itself, or perish with the passengers ; and that, to enable it to reach the desired port in safety, it is glorious to rally with brethren who know how to fight, to conquer, and forgive. For my part, convinced as I am that our divisions constitute the joy and the hope of our enemies ; persuaded that this region is the only one which is still at the service of free minds ; assured by experience that the cause of the black and of the yellow is one and indivisible; and acquainted by ample proof of the new plots that are framing by our common tyrants to render our quarrels of endless duration ; I call upon God and upon men to witness, that no sacrifice shall be too dear for me that can tend to reunite the children of Hayti under the paternal shield.—Trusting in my own means, and confident of the legitimacy of my cause, which give strength to my ascendancy, I do not hesitate to renew here the *general amnesty* which I have already offered, to promote the welfare of the state, the only object of my ambition.

But, if it be desirable that one portion of the Haytians, who are still under the influence of error, should relinquish that error, and expiate the wrongs of many years by a moment of repentance, it is for the public advantage that the members of the great family should reunite, to the consternation and despair of our tyrants, and not the less necessary to preserve that attitude which befits men, who, having done much, are aware that there still remains much more for them to do.

SOLDIERS,

YOU are about to return to your respective garrisons and cantonments, to refresh yourselves after the toilsome fatigues you have undergone; carry with you that sense of order, of subordination and discipline which is the sacred pledge of victory.

It is my intention to distribute the rewards of valour to those who have distinguished themselves by their good deeds: your corps are about to be completed, and clothed and equipped anew; enjoy then in peace the fruit of your laurels, and be ready, at the first signal, to complete the triumph of the legitimate authority.

Done at our Palace of Cape Henry, the 8th October 1810, in the seventh year of the independence of Hayti.

HENRY CHRISTOPHE.

By the President,

The Field Marshal, and private Secretary of his Serene Highness,

PREVOST.

With mixed sentiments of affection and transport the President was received on his return from the campaign: every one flocked to scatter before his feet the laurels of victory; and from Port de Paix to Henry there were nothing but triumphal arches and trophies, raised by the emulative delights of the people. His progress was in fact the whole way a triumphal march. How delightful, how honourable to be thus beloved! but how pleasing besides to have such worthy citizens who think the same!

The war being happily terminated, and the north entirely cleared of enemies, the troops were sent back to their homes, to enjoy that repose of which they had so much need.

Receive, ye brave and faithful troops who acknowledge the legitimate authority, a tribute of admiration, and the homage of respect from one of your companions in arms, who knows the spirit of a soldier, who delights in being in the midst of you, who has sometimes shared your dangers, and to whom your lots can never be a matter of indifference. The God of battles has blessed and crowned your arms with glory. Thanks be to you! you have delivered your countrymen from the fury of civil war and of anarchy; you have doubtless done much, but you think nothing done so long as it remains for you to plant your victorious standards in every quarter which rebellion may defile.

The President, not yet recovered from the fatigues at the Mole, applied himself next to the organization of the forces, both land and naval; he passes the troops in review, has the muster roll of names called over, causes all accounts to be settled down to the last soldier of every regiment, sends back to the labours of cultivation such as he does not think proper to be retained in the service, replaces them with young recruits, nominates to vacant places, completes the regiments and crews, has the arms of the troops repaired and placed in a proper state, as well as the vessels of the squadron : he clothes the army, and provisions the fleet for a cruise.

He organizes in a legion the troops of the South that surrendered at the Mole, appoints to the vacant places in this corps, and gives them rank in the army. Undeceived of their errors, he no longer considers them otherwise than as his children.

He engages in a plan of farming out the demesnes; and in the distribution of farms he is not unmindful of those unfortunate widows and hapless orphans whom the fate of war or the course of nature has deprived of a husband, of a tender father ; he replaces the want of this tender father to these interesting creatures, not only in securing their maintenance, but by procuring for them the benefits of an education, which is equivalent to replacing, for the country, the authors of their being!

The President then visits the provinces. He is received throughout, not as

the conqueror of the Mole, but like a vivi-
fying genius come to visit those parts.
His ameliorating eye embraces all sides.
He has the sweet satisfaction of seeing
that the cultivators, being every where regularly paid by a fourth of the gross produce, were praising the freedom they enjoyed. If unjust and rapacious farmers
no more deprive them of the wages of
their labour, and grow rich by the sweat
of their brow; if cattle are allowed to
ravage no more their gardens and provision grounds; if the banana is allowed
to ripen on the banana tree, it is to Henry
that these men of nature are indebted for
it. He it is who animates industry, and
gives life to commerce. In his presence
the people vent their exclamations of joy,
the unequivocal returns of a degree of
affection and attachment bordering upon
idolatry. From his palace he descends
into the lowly cottage of the cultivator, as
into the soldier's hut, and their happiness

is at all times the constant object of his most lively and tenderest solicitude.

The re-establishment of manners, which now become the order of the day, imparted its influence on the peace and comfort of families. Vice disappeared, and hid its corrupt practices; the sacred tie of marriage was respected, that tender union which binds man to woman, creates virtuous companions, and attaches the citizen to his country, the great family of the state, by the image of his own and of domestic happiness; as the greatest encouragement to which, the supreme head furnishes, himself, a touching example of the conjugal virtues: he proves that good manners are the attendants of good monarchs, and constitute the glory of their reign; as, on the other hand, from licentiousness come bad princes, to the disgrace of their government.

The President thought to yield to the dictates of his generous breast, which was

affected with the calamities of civil war:
in the midst of victory he sacrifices his re-
sentments. Forgetful of his offers and promises of peace having been so frequently
despised, he thought it due to his citizens,
in order to convince them still more fully
of his intentions, to dispatch commissioners empowered to treat for peace with the
revolted Petion at Port aux Crimes; these
commissioners were followed by a deputa-
tion of twelve military men from the different corps of the South, who surrendered at the Mole, for the purpose of informing their comrades of the treatment they
had experienced. It was natural to expect that offers of sincerity like these
would have been properly appreciated, as
they ought to have been; and all good
citizens began already to flatter themselves with a hope of the war being terminated. Vain hope! that dream is fled;
the mind of the president is now the more
persuaded, that it is only by the adoption

I

of rigorous measures, as at the Cape, that he can expect to triumph over the too guilty infatuation of the revolters!

I pass with satisfaction from this detail of our grievances, and now arrive at the most interesting part of my work.

Genius of my country, inspire my understanding! Truth, it is under thy auspices I have taken up the pen. Deign to direct it still, that my writings, animated by thy sublime eloquence, may carry into the remotest climes the glory and the virtue of a Henry, that his beloved name may never be pronounced abroad but with the veneration which it inspires; and that, instructed in his good qualities, and by the recital of what he has done for his people and for posterity, all foreigners may at length agree, that in the lot of this class of mankind, hitherto groaning under the yoke of prejudices, there are found to be, as among them, those extraordinary beings, evidently under the protection of nature and of Heaven, who are to appear in the revolutions of this world to heal their afflictions, and restore social order to those limits from which the impetuous course of events had chased it!

The Haytians had just celebrated the eighth year of their independence; and if the dawn of that beautiful day did not as yet witness their reunion, at least they were abundantly persuaded by the great achievements that Henry had accomplished, to hope, that he alone had the will as well as the power to consolidate and strengthen the foundations of that independence, so earnestly to be desired.

For some time the declared opinion of the most respectable and enlightened citizens was in favour of placing Henry on the throne; they had known the insufficiency of the title with which they had invested him in calamitous times. The chief of a warlike nation, who ought never to forget that, the moment when that nation lays aside its warlike character, will be that when it will run the risk of its existence being annihilated, or rather that its existence is essentially connected with its martial ardour; this Chief, I say, will not long be able to maintain the character of a dignity which does not associate with it the idea of the sovereign power: the revision of the constitution was therefore decided upon. The council of state applied itself with zeal to this purpose; but its labours which were directed to the offering of a monument of the gratitude and acknowledgement of all good Haytians, by adjudging the crown to Henry, and making it hereditary in his illlustrious house, could not remain secret. It transpired, when he was on a journey to Fort Dauphin, the 26th March, a day for ever celebrated, when the head of the state was hailed and proclaimed King, his august spouse Queen of Hayti, and their son Prince Royal. The happy news once spread, communicated with the rapidity of the electric flame; and the general assent of all classes of society, proved that this good and magnanimous people foresaw the propriety of so great and glorious an event; it is needless to observe, that their majesties were received with unbounded transports of affection and joy on their arrival in the capital. It was to no purpose they entered it by night: they found all the people stirring, eager to lavish upon them those marks of respect, and those congratulations, which carry with them such sincerity and feeling when they proceed from the heart. Their majesties received, the same night, the felicitations and homage of all the civil and military bodies, as well as those of the foreign merchants established in the capital, who thought it their duty to pay this tribute of respect and veneration to their majesties.

The council of state having formed

itself into a general council, and having accordingly invited to the meeting all the principal officers of the land and sea forces, and such of the principal citizens as were considered worthy of being ad⤸ mitted to the deliberations, to give them more eclat, then put the finishing stroke to their immortal work, and proceeded in grand convocation, the 4th April, to the palace of their majesties. Being presented by the grand master of the ceremonies to their majesties, who were surrounded by their royal family; his excellency Lieutenant General Paul Romain, the organ of the general council, expressed himself in the following terms:

" The council of state has the honour to present to your Majesty the law of the constitution, the completion of which has been the object of its most profound meditations.

We shall have fulfilled the expectations of the people and of the army, and our labours will have corresponded with the wish of our hearts, if the fundamental basis on which this new kingdom is about to rest, is happily calculated to reconcile public happiness with the majesty of the throne, and the dignity of the national representation.

This day of everlasting memory on which the Haytian people are to acknowledge, in the face of heaven and of earth, their protector, their father, and their king, in the person of that generous being who has saved them, impresses our minds with the most delightful emotions.

At the sight of the diadem which is about to rest on that august front whereon our glorious destinies are inscribed, tremble, ye enemies of our country! This moment has for ever decided on the sovereignty of these realms, and it is that of a triumph for all hearts, since at length they have crowned the idol of their choice.

To the valiant arm of Henry the sceptre belongs; it is the attribute of true courage; and fortune, ever attentive to the voice of genius, assigns to him, at this moment, the reward of twenty years of labour.

Hayti, erect thy proud head; be no more alarmed respecting thy future prosperity, and offer up to Heaven a return of thanks; for, when a Henry ascends the throne, the days of Sully are about to re-appear."

His Majesty replied:

" GENTLEMEN,

" I have no other happiness than that of the people of Hayti, of whose toils I have partaken; and nothing that interests the welfare of the state can be indifferent to me.

The nation has judged necessary to its prosperity and safety to elevate me to the throne, and to fix the hereditary succession in my family; I yield to its wish, since it contributes to the public felicity.

This day, in giving me the measure of all hearts, will never cease to be present to my mind; it will recall to me all that the Haytian people hath done for me and my family, and every moment of my life shall be devoted to recompensing it for its filial tenderness.

I will be on the throne, the same as I have been in adversity, and such as becomes a good king to be; and may my descendants inherit successively that pure affection with which my heart throbs for my country!"

Then his Excellency Lieutenant General Paul Romain, addressing himself to her Majesty the Queen, said,

" MADAM,

" We have just had the honour of presenting to your august spouse the law of the constitution, which for ever fixes the destiny of Hayti, at the same time that it renders hereditary, in the family of our sovereign, the monarchy of the state.

If any thing can add to the gratifying sensations that animate our hearts, it is to see the eminent qualities Heaven has bestowed upon you, raised to that throne which the affection and acknowledgment of the Haytians has prepared for you.

Eternal thanks be to the Almighty, who seems never to have raised so high such sense and goodness of which your heart is the sanctuary, unless for purposes of more extended influence over that country on which they are shed.

The Council of State delights in placing at the feet of your Majesty the tribute of love, of respect, of gratitude, and admiration, which your virtues are so well calculated to inspire."

Her Majesty replied:

" GENTLEMEN,

"The appellation of Queen, which the nation has just decreed to me, unites me more closely with the fortunes of the Haytian people, to whom I delight in being a tender mother.

I shall never be unmindful, whilst on the throne, of the duties which the Royal Majesty enjoins; and seeing my family is destined hereafter to take my place, it will be my pleasing duty to superintend their education with peculiar care, so that my children may be to me my dearest decorations, as on them will one day depend the destiny of my country."

CONSTITUTIONAL LAW

OF THE

COUNCIL OF STATE

Which establishes Royalty in Hayti.

THE Council of State, at an extraordinary meeting held for the purpose of deliberating upon the alterations which it is necessary to introduce in the state of Hayti, and on the form of government most suitable thereto ;

Considering that, when the constitution of the 17th of February 1807, anno 4, was promulgated, the state found itself in fact without any social compact; and the storms of civil contention raged with such fury, as not to permit the representatives of the people to fix in a permanent manner the only mode of government which is really adapted to us ;

That this constitution, notwithstanding all the informality which it appeared to consist of, and its numerous imperfections, of which the representatives themselves were not unaware, was yet suited at that time to the crisis which gave it birth, and the tempests then hovering over its infancy. That the few great principles of which it consisted were nevertheless sufficient for the happiness of the people, in securing all their rights in those deplorable times.

Considering, that at the present period, thanks to the genius of the supreme Magistrate who holds the reins of government, whose elevated conceptions and brilliant valour have prevailed in restoring order, happiness, and prosperity; the flourishing state of cultivation, of trade and navigation; the re-establishment of manners, religion, and morality; the high discipline observed in the army and the fleet; seem to promise a lasting duration to the state. That it becomes us at present, more than ever, to establish a fixed order of things, a mode of government calculated to rule at all times the country that gave us birth.

Considering that it is urgently necessary to invest the sovereign authority with a character great and august, so as to convey an idea of the supremacy of power;

That the erection of an hereditary throne is the necessary consequence of this forcible consideration;

That the inheritance of power to be vested only as to the male legitimate children (to the perpetual exclusion of females) in an illustrious family, constantly devoted to the glory and happiness of the country, which owes its political existence to it, is as much a duty as a signal mark of national acknowledgment.

That it is the nation which now exercises, through us, its will and its sovereignty, in confiding them to him who has rescued it from that abyss in which its most inveterate enemies would extinguish it, to him who governs it with so much glory, that this nation has nothing to fear for its liberty, its independence, and its happiness.

That it is necessary also to establish high dignities, as well to uphold the splendour of the throne as to reward eminent services rendered to the country by officers who devote themselves to the happiness, the glory, and prosperity of the state.

The Council of State, therefore, enacts, in consequence, the Organic Law following ;

ACT I.

Of the Supreme Authority.

ARTICLE I.

THE President, Henry Christophe, is declared King of Hayti, under the name of Henry.

This title, with its prerogatives and privileges, shall be hereditary in the male and legitimate descendants of his family in a direct line, by elder birthright, to the exclusion of females.

Art. 2. All the acts of the kingdom shall be in the name of the King, published and promulgated under the royal seal.

Art. 3. In default of male children in a direct line, the succession shall pass into the family of the Prince nearest akin to the sovereign, or the most ancient in dignity.

Art. 4. Meanwhile, it shall be lawful for the King to adopt the children of such Prince of the kingdom as he shall judge proper, in default of an heir-apparent.

Art. 5. In the event of there happening to be, subsequent to the adoption, male children, their right of succession shall prevail over that of the adopted children.

Art. 6. At the decease of the King, and until his succession is acknowledged, the affairs of the kingdom shall be governed by the ministers and the King's Council, who shall jointly form a general council: their decisions to be determined by a majority of voices. The secretary of state to keep a record of the deliberations.

ACT II.

Of the Royal Family.

Art. 7. The King's spouse is declared Queen of Hayti.

Art. 8. The members of the royal family shall bear the title of Princes and Princesses; they are to be styled Royal Highnesses. The heir-apparent denominated Prince Royal.

Art. 9. The Princes are to take their seats as members of the council of state, on their coming of age.

K

Art. 10. The Royal Princes and Princesses cannot marry without the approbation of the King.

Art. 11. The King himself directs the organization of his palace in a manner conformable to the dignity of the crown.

Art. 12. There shall be established, after the orders of the King, palaces and castles in those parts of the kingdom which he shall judge proper to fix upon.

ACT III.

Of the Regency.

Art. 13. The King is a minor until he shall have completed his fifteenth year : during his minority he shall be styled a Regent of the kingdom.

Art. 14. The Protector shall be at least twenty-five years of age, and shall be chosen from among the Princes most nearly related to the King (to the exclusion of females), and in default of such, from among the great dignitaries of the kingdom.

Art. 15. In default of the appointment of a protector on the part of the King, the general council will select one in the manner prescribed in the foregoing article.

Art. 16. The protector exercises, until the King comes of age, all the attributes of the royal dignity.

Art. 17. He cannot conclude any treaty of peace, alliance, or commerce, nor make any declaration of war until after mature deliberation, and the advice of the general council : their opinions shall be taken according to the majority of votes ; and in case of equality, that side which is found to be conformable to the opinion of the protector, shall preponderate.

Art. 18. The protector cannot nominate either to the great dignities of the kingdom or to the situations of general officers in the land and sea forces.

Art. 19. All the acts of the regency are in the name of the King, who is minor.

Art. 20. The care of the King, during his minority, is confided to his mother, and in default of her, to the prince appointed by the late King.

Neither the protector, nor his descendants, shall be eligible for the charge of the King, who is minor.

ACT IV.

Of the Great Council, and of the Privy Council.

Art. 21. The great council is composed of the princes of the blood, of princes, dukes, and counts, nominated and chosen by his Majesty, who himself fixes their number.

Art. 22. The King presides at the council, and when he does not preside in person, he fixes upon one of the dignitaries of the kingdom to fulfil that office.

Art. 23. The privy council is chosen by the King from among the great dignitaries of the kingdom.

ACT V.

Of the Great Officers of the Kingdom.

Art. 24. The great officers of the kingdom are grand marshals of Hayti: they are chosen from among the generals of all ranks, according to merit.

Art. 25. Their number is not limited ; the King determines upon it at every promotion.

Art. 26. The places of great officers of the kingdom are for life.

Art. 27. When, by the King's order, or on account of being invalided, any one of the great officers of the kingdom shall cease to be actively employed, he shall nevertheless retain his titles, his rank, and the half of his pay.

ACT VI.

Of the Ministry.

Art. 28. There shall be in the kingdom four ministers chosen and appointed by the King:

The minister of war and marine,

The minister of finances and of the interior,

The minister of foreign affairs,

and

The minister of justice.

Art. 29. The ministers are members of the council, and have a deliberative voice.

Art. 30. The ministers account directly to his Majesty, and receive his orders.

ACT VII.

Of the Oaths.

Art. 31. The King at his accession, or on his coming of age, takes an oath upon the Gospels, in presence of the great authorities of the kingdom.

Art. 32. The protector, before undertaking the exercise of his functions, also takes an oath, with the same formalities.

Art. 33. The principal clergy, the great officers, the ministers, and the secretary of state, also take the oath of fidelity at the King's hands.

ACT VIII.

Of the Promulgation.

Art. 34. The promulgation of all the acts of the kingdom is thus couched:

WE, by the grace of God and the constitutional law of the state, King of Hayti, to all present and to come, greeting.

And all public acts will conclude thus :

WE do hereby order and command, that these presents, sealed with our seal, be addressed to all courts, tribunals, and administrative authorities, to be transcribed in their registers, to be observed and caused to be observed throughout the kingdom; and the minister of justice is charged with the promulgation thereof.

Art. 35. The executory proceedings in judgments of the courts of justice and of the tribunals, are to run thus :

WE, by the grace of God and of the constitutional law of the state, King of Hayti, to all present and to come, greeting.

Then follows the copy of the judgment or decree : " We order and command all constables and other officers, on this requisition, to put in execution the said judgment, and our attorneys in the tribunals to promote the same; and the commandants and officers of the public force to assist, whensoever they may be legally required so to do.

In testimony of which the present judgment has been signed by the president of the court, and the register.

Done by the council of state of Hayti, at Cape Henry, the 28th March, 1811, the 8th year of independence.

SIGNED——*Paul Romain, senior; Andrew Vernet, Touissant Brave, Jean Philippe, Daux, Martial Besse, Jean Pierre Richard, Jean Fleury, Jean Baptiste Juge, Etienne Magny, Secretary.*

We, the apostolic Prefect, and the general officers of the army and navy, the administrators of the finances, and officers of justice undersigned, as well in our own names as in the names of the army and the people, of which we are here the representatives, do join, in heart and soul, with the council of state, for the proclamation of his majesty *Henry Christophe*, king of Hayti, such being our wish and that of the people, and of the army, for a long time past.

C. Brelle, Apostolic Prefect; N. Joachim Rouanez, Lieut. Generals; Pierre Touissant, Raphael, Louis Achille, Charles Carlot, Cottereau, Jasmin, Prevost, Dupont, Charles Pierre, Guerrier, Simon, Placide Lebrun, Field Marshals; Bastien, Jean Baptiste, Pierre St. Jean, Rear Admirals; Almanjor jun. Henry Proix, Chevalier, Papalier, Raimond, Sicard, Ferrier, Dosson, Caze, Brigadier Generals; Bastien Fabien, Cadet Antoine, Bernardine Sprew, Commanders in the Navy; Stanislas, Latortue, Joseph Latortue, Comptrollers; Delon, Inspector; Jean Baptiste, Petit Treasurer; P. A. Charrier, Director of Domains; L. Raphael, Director of Customs; Boyer, Keeper of the Central Warehouse; Juste

Hugonin, Commissary General of Govern-ment ; Isaac, Justice of the Peace ; Lagrone, Charlatte, Notaries; Dupuy, Interpreter of Government.

The 6th of April was the day chosen for the publication of the constitution. The council of state in grand assembly; the commissary general of government, bearing the original of the constitutional law; the governor of the capital, the officers of the staff, and those of the regiments in garrison at the capital; the officers of administration, the members of the tribunals, the advocates; the principle merchants of Hayti, and foreigners; besides a multitude of respectable citizens of all ranks and degrees, mixed and blended together, all animated with the liveliest joy, which was depicted in their looks, then repaired, at the sound of warlike music, to all the public places and cross-ways, and heard read to them copies of the address from the council of state to the people, as follows.

The Council of State, to the People, and to the Army and Navy of Hayti.

FELLOW CITIZENS,

Your representatives are once more assembled for the purpose of revising the constitution of Hayti, of the 17th February, 1807, Anno 4. Having to pronounce upon your dearest interests, they have done so with all the zeal and patriotism of which they are capable. To justify your confidence, they have called upon the most enlightened Haytians; they have matured, in the silence of the cabinet, that form of government which is adapted to the country that gave us birth; they have never lost sight of your happiness, with which they are indispensably connected, and now present to you the fruit of their labours.

When the state, menaced by the con-

spiracies which were formed in its very
breast, and lighted up by our cruel and inveterate enemies, presented only a picture
of chaos and general disorder, the great
man who governs us perceived the necessity of a social pact, around which might
unite all those Haytians for whom the
name of country is not an empty sound:
he convoked us, and we hastened to second
his views, and to offer to you the code of
laws, which has now been amended.

We did not at that time disguise the
fact that this work was not entirely accomplished: we thought that the principles we
proclaimed might at least suffice for the
crisis in which we found ourselves; and
seeing the storms that raged around the
vessel of the state, we reserved to ourselves
the care of retouching our work, of perfecting and adapting it still more to our
customs, our manners, and our laws. In
this flattering hope, we waited till the tem-
pest being allayed, and the sky more se-

rene, might allow of our resuming the course of our labours.

Thanks to the tutelary genius of Hayti, thanks to the supreme magistrate; thanks to his elevated conceptions, his brilliant valour, his energy, his activity. Victory, faithful to his arms, has seated itself beneath his colours; tranquillity reappears, order is established; discipline has been permanently restored in the army and in the fleet; conspiracies have been suppressed; the conspirators punished; justice has resumed its course; morals and public instruction have been reformed; cultivation and commerce have been bettered; at length, happiness and prosperity have appeared once more, and promise a lasting duration to the state; this we have thought the happy occasion for perfecting the institutions which we had but roughly commenced, and we said to ourselves, the time is now come.

In order to preserve ourselves from

those violent checks, those horrible convul-
sions which have so often agitated and
overturned this body politic; to curb that
ebb and flow of passion, those plots of intrigue, the fury of factions, and the reac-
tion of parties; in a word, to shun for ever
that chaos, that confusion and perpetual
clashing which result from those monstrous
associations known under the name of
popular bodies; we have felt the necessity
of having one sole and supreme head,
under whose powerful protection there shall
be no more collision: our hearts have
been in unison with those of the people
and of the army, who have conceived that
the government of one individual is the
most natural, the least subject to troubles
and reverses, and such as unites, in a supreme degree, the power of maintaining
our laws, protecting our rights, defending
our liberty, and making us respected
abroad.

But it was not enough to invest the

sovereign authority with a character grand
and imposing, such as to give an idea of
the majesty of power, to impress that respect inseparable from the royal authority,
but which gave all the latitude possible for
doing good, in recognising only the law
to be subservient to his will; it was necessary moreover, in the event of a vacancy
in the throne, to consider the best method
to be observed, in order to obviate those
interminable civil broils, to maintain tranquillity, and the stability of the body politic, when hereditary succession appeared
to us the most suitable to this important
end.

Passing from these high considerations
to others essential for the purpose of conferring splendour upon the throne, we have
been occupied with instituting an hereditary
nobility, whose honour is to be their dis-
tinguishing character; whose fidelity must
be above all proof; their devotion unbounded, and their resolution inflexible to

conquer or die in defence of that throne from which they derive their primitive lustre.

We have analyzed the powers, the attributes and denominations assigned in every part of the world to these superior beings, born evidently to command their species ; but accountable, at the same time, to the Supreme One, for all the benefits or evils that may result from their administration ; and by our study of the characters of those who have held the government of our island since we took up arms in defence of our rights, and finally since the expulsion of our enemies, and the proclamation of our independence, we have considered, that the title of Governor-general conferred upon the pious, the upright commander in chief, Toussaint Louverture of glorious memory, and afterwards upon the immortal founder of our independence, was in no wise adapted to the dignity of the supreme magistrate, inas-

much as it seemed that such a denomina-
tion would be only suitable at most to an
officer in the pay of any power whatever :
on the other hand, the magnificent title of
Emperor, given to the general in chief
Dessalines, although worthy indeed of
being offered to such a man, after the
eminent services he had rendered to the
state, and to his fellow citizens, yet wanted justness in its application. An emperor is considered to take the lead of other
sovereigns ; or at least, so exalted a dignity
supposes in the possessor of it, not only
the same power, and the same dominion,
but moreover a real and effective command over different states and territories.
Again, the temporary title of President
given to his successor, the great Henry,
our august chief, does not convey the idea
of supreme power, and can only be applicable in an assemblage of men met together, where the exercise of those functions is necessary, or in a judicial body.

The example of the United States, governed by a president, does not alter our
opinion as to the insufficiency of this title;
the Americans, having succeeded in adopt-
ing the federative system, may, as a new
people, approve of their present government; but we have carried our views
further: and though we appear in the
same hypothetical situation as the Americans, being a new people, still we possess
the wants, the manners, the virtues, and
we will add, the vices of the old states.
Of all the modes of government, that which
has appeared to us most justly deserving of
a preference, is one of a middle tenor,
between those hitherto put in practice at
Hayti: we have observed, with the great
Montesquieu,* the excellence of a paternal
monarchial government over other governments. The extent of the territory of
Hayti is more than sufficient for the for-
mation of a kingdom: many of the Euro-

* Montesquieu, Esprit des Lois, Chap. XI.

pean states, acknowledged by all the established powers, have neither the same extent, the same resources, the same wealth, nor the same population. We say nothing as to the same martial valour and heroic character of the Haytian people : its glory is known throughout the world !

The establishment of a throne, hereditary in the family of that great man who has governed this state with so much renown, has, therefore, appeared to us necessary, as a sacred and imperious duty, as well as a signal mark of the national gratude. The purity of his intentions, the fidelity of his soul, are to us infallible guarantees that the Haytian people will have nothing to fear for their liberties, their independence, or their felicity The natural consequence of the establishment of the throne has been the foundation of a rank of hereditary nobility, into which might be admitted all such distinguished citizens as have rendered important services to the state, whether in the magistracy, in the profession of arms, or in science and letters. It has been our wish to add to the splendour of the throne by this illustrious institution, which will tend in itself to excite a generous emulation, and a heartfelt devotion to the service of the prince and of the kingdom.

If, to justify our choice, it were necessary to cite examples, we should find them numerous in history. How many great men, the sole artizans of their own fortune, by the aid alone of their genius, by the vigour of their understanding, have founded empires, and extended wide their boundaries; have given to their people the precious advantages of a society wisely ordered, together with a taste for knowledge, and the arts of civilized life. Without going further back, we may look at the striking instance which presents itself to all his cotemporaries, of that extraordinary man, our implacable enemy; he,

whose every thought meditates our destruction, and who at this time reigns with
such absolute sway in Europe; what
was he prior to the commencement of
that celebrated revolution, to the issue
of which he owes his rapid elevation? Nothing but a slender reed,
whose fragile and precarious existence
was then to all appearance very remote
from attaining such an exalted degree of
glory and of power. Like those who
raised him to the highest rank, we now
exercise the privileges of men, which we
derive from nature: after having re-con-
quered our rights, our liberty, and our independence, it is our will to found, in this
new world, an Hereditary Monarchy: we
hasten to decide at length the, hitherto
uncertain, destinies of this country, by
declaring that Henry is invested with the
sovereign authority, that the throne is
hereditary in his family, and that the happiness of Haytians is to be dated from the

period of the foundation of sovereign power in these territories.

Fellow Citizens, in adjusting the fundamental bases of the kingdom which we have erected, we believe we have merited the great confidence you thought proper to place in us. If a few envious or pusillanimous traducers stand up against these new institutions we have adopted, we answer, that it is time to dispel all remains of any hope our enemies may still entertain. Should these same enemies not have profited by the terrible experience they have acquired, and should they, in the blindness of their rage, again pollute our soil with their bloodthirsty battalions, may they find at their approach a united people, who have already made a trial of their strength ; inured to martial discipline through intestine divisions, familiarised to danger and to war ; a nation armed and ready to dispute with them the country they would invade ! they will

find a distinguished monarch, ranking
among the worthies of the 19th century,
oftentimes crowned with laurels of victory,
now re-united, and surrounded with his
faithful nobles, ready to brave every
danger, to perish for the safety of his
people, and rather to bury himself under
the ruins of his throne than crouch beneath an ignominious yoke. May the
happy people of beauteous Hayti, so
favoured by nature, reunite with each
other around the constitutional law, a law
which regard for their happiness, our only
aim, first suggested ; may they swear to
defend it, and then we shall be competent
to withstand all the tyrants in the universe.

Fellow Citizens, we shall be abundantly
rewarded for our toils, if, in the secure
possession of your rights, you shall find, in
deriving from them all the happiness
which we have been desirous of enabling
you to enjoy, new motives of attachment

to the government of our common
country.

Done at Cape Henry, the 4th April,
1811, the eighth year of independence.

Signed,

Paul Romain, sen. André Vernet, Toussaint Brave, Jean Philip Daux, Martial Besse, Jean Pierre Richard, Jean Fleury, Jean Baptiste Juge, Etienne Magnay, secretary.

Immediately after this address, the
Constitutional Act was read over to the
people, who received the same with loud
and repeated acclamations of " Long
live the King, long live the Queen, the
Prince, and Royal Family!"

In the course of a short time the public
edicts of government, directing the organization of the new form of government,
successively made their appearance, and
the celerity of their publication did not
detract from the wisdom of their contents.

KINGDOM OF HAYTI.

Manifesto of the King.

Sovereign of a nation too long oppressed, a nation which has suffered cruel persecution, and which, by its energy, its perseverance, its valour, and its prowess, has succeeded in acquiring, by the sword, liberty and independence ; the only object of our constant solicitude, of our incessant labours, for the happiness of the virtuous, brave, and generous people, who have confided to us their destinies, has always been, to give it a place within the pale of civilized nations.

It is under the present favourable circumstances, now that liberal and healing opinions seem to efface the memory of those disastrous times, when the people groaned under oppression; now that we see the Sovereigns of Europe busied about the welfare of their subjects; that we deem it our duty to elevate our voice, to justify, before the tribunal of nations, the legitimacy of our independence.

A simple statement of facts, a plain narrative of the events which have led to our independence, will suffice to prove to demonstration, to the universe at large, our rights and the justice of our cause.

We will not attempt to give a sketch of the deplorable situation into which we were plunged before the epocha of our emancipation; the world knows how, for the space of more than a hundred and fifty years, we groaned under the frightful yoke of slavery, doomed to contempt and suffering. The tale of our long misfortunes, and the picture of the horrible tortures that we have endured beneath the colonial system, are the province of our history, which will transmit them to posterity.

We hasten to emerge from this period of disgrace and iniquity, to arrive at the epoch when universal liberty was pro- claimed by the agents of the French go- vernment, and sanctioned by France her- self, during many years of connexion and communication, of mutual and uninter- rupted correspondence, between the go- vernments of the two countries.

We merited the blessings of liberty, by our loyal attachment to the mother coun- try; we evinced our gratitude when, reduced to our own resources, deprived of all com- munication with the parent state, we re- sisted every seduction ; when, inflexible to menaces, deaf to propositions, inacces- sible to artifice, we braved misery, fa- mine, privations of every description, and finally triumphed over her numerous enemies, as well internal as external.

We were then far from anticipating, as a reward for so much constancy and such sacrifices of our blood, that, after the lapse of twelve years, and in a manner the most barbarous, France would desire to ravish from us that most precious of all possessions, Liberty.

Under the administration of the Governor General, Toussaint Louverture, Hayti was regenerating from her ashes; every thing seemed to promise us a happy futurity. The arrival of General Hedouville made a total change in the aspect of affairs, and gave a mortal blow to public tranquillity. We will not enter into the details of his intrigues with the Haytian General Rigaud, and how he succeeded in persuading him to rebel against his legitimate chief; we shall go no further than to say, that, before he quitted the island, this agent effected the subversion of all order, by spreading among us the brands of discord, and lighting up the torch of civil war; and that it was not till torrents of blood had been shed, that tranquillity could be re-established.

Always intent upon the work of restoration, the Governor, Toussaint Louverture, under his paternal administration,
had reinstated, in full force, law, morals,
religion, education, and industry ; agriculture and commerce were flourishing. He
favoured the white colonists, particularly
the planters. Indeed, his attentions and
partialities had been carried to such a
length, that he was loudly blamed for entertaining more affection for them than
for those of his own colour. Nor was this
reproach without foundation ; for, a few
months before the arrival of the French, he
immolated his own nephew, General
Moyse, who had disregarded the orders he
had given for the protection of the colonists. That act of the governor, added to
the great confidence he had placed in the
French authorities, was the principal cause
of the feeble resistance the French encoun-
tered in Hayti. Indeed, his confidence
in these authorities was such, that he had

discharged the greater part of the regular troops, and sent them back to the tillage of the soil.

Such was the situation of things, when the peace of Amiens was negociating. It was hardly concluded, before a formidable armament disembarked upon the whole extent of our coasts a numerous army, which took us by surprise at the moment we thought ourselves in the most perfect security, and plunged us at once into an abyss of calamity.

Posterity will scarcely credit, that in an enlightened age, when philanthropy was generally diffused among mankind, an enterprise so abominable should ever have taken place. It was from the midst of an intelligent people that this swarm of barbarians issued forth with the criminal design of exterminating a civilized and peaceable nation, or replunging them for ever in slavery and bondage.

It was not enough to come with a

strong hand ; it was necessary, the better
to insure success to the expedition, to employ perfidious and infamous means; it was
necessary to sow disunion amongst us, as
a salutary diversion in favour of their destructive projects. They neglected nothing
to attain their execrable ends. The chiefs
of both colours who were to be found in
France, the sons of the Governor Louverture himself, were pressed into the service
for the expedition. They were, like ourselves, cajoled by the proclamation of the
First Consul, a masterpiece of perfidy, in
which he told us, " *You are all equal and
free before God and before the Republic."*
At the same time that the instructions of
General Leclerc were expressly in favour
of slavery. It was not enough to call
upon men to witness his falsehood, but
the Divinity too must be insulted by this
horrible and blasphemous appeal.

The major part of the population, deceived by fallacious promises, accustomed

for ages to consider themselves as French, submitted without resistance. So little did the governor himself expect to have any enemy to combat, that he had given no orders to his general to resist, in case of attack. When the French squadron was descried, he was making the circuit of the eastern side of the island ; if some generals resisted, it was only in consequence of the menaces and hostile manner of summoning them to surrender, which made them take counsel of their duty, their honour, and the circumstances in which they were placed.

As evidence of the truth of these assertions, we refer to the original documents, printed and annexed to these presents, from No. 1 to 14 inclusively.

After some months resistance, the Governor General yielded to the pressing entreaties of General Leclerc, and to his solemn protestations that the maintenance of liberty was the basis of his instructions,

M

and that France would never violate its most beautiful work. Peace was negotiated with the French on this footing, and the Governor Toussaint resigned his authority, and retired peaceably to the retreat which he had chosen.

Scarcely had the French succeeded in extending their dominion over the whole island, more by cunning and persuasion than by the force of thair arms, when they began to put in execution their frightful system of slavery and destruction.

As a step towards this object, they resolved to arrest Governor Toussaint Louverture ; they forged a correspondence, (composed by mercenary and machiavelian scribblers) ; they imputed to him designs which never entered his head ; they kidnapped him from his habitation at Pongaudin, while reposing in the full faith of treaties ; loaded with fetters, he was dragged, with his family, on board the *Hero* and transported to France. All Europe knows how he terminated his unfortunate career in the torments and horrors of the dungeons of the Chateau de Joux, in Franche-Comté.

Such was the reward bestowed on his attachment, and the great and eminent services he had rendered to France and the colonists.

That moment was the signal of arrests throughout the whole extent of the island. All those who had shewn strength of soul, of intellect, or of character, at the time when we vindicated the rights of man, were the first to be laid hold of; they spared not even the traitors who most contributed to the success of the French armies, by informing and conducting their advanced guards, and themselves marking down and arresting their fellow-citizens. At first they offered them for sale in the foreign colonies; failing in this project, they resolved to convey them to France, where labour in the galleys, and in the highways, fetters, or dungeons, awaited them.

It was then that the white colonists, whose numbers progressively increased, believing their power already confirmed, threw off the mask of dissimulation, loudly declared the reestablishment of slavery, and took their measures accordingly. These men had the impudence to claim, as their slaves, citizens, men who had recommended themselves by the signal services they had rendered their country, as well in a civil as in a military capacity; virtuous and upright magistrates; warriors covered with scars, whose blood had flowed in the cause of France and liberty, were again subjected to the yoke of slavery. These colonists, scarcely reseated in their estates, affected all those airs of haughtiness with which insolent masters always treat their slaves. While their power yet hung upon a thread, they already marked out and selected those whom they designed to be the first victims sacrificed to their revenge.

Then arrived the infamous decree of Bonaparte, which confirmed the reestablishment of slavery. The better to insult our misery, he also employed towards us the same mystic jargon which he used towards the people of Europe; for it was to him habitual. This decree was brought us by a traitor, who had sold himself; in short, by Hercules, a black officer; to sum up all, his slave.

The proud and *liberticide* faction of the colonists, and dealers in human flesh, which, since the commencement of the Revolution, has worried all the successive governments of France with their plans, projects, most extravagant and atrocious memorials, all tending to our destruction; this faction, tormented by the remembrance of the despotism which it had exercised in Hayti, agitated by a whirlwind of different passions, employed every means that could be devised, to regain the prey that had escaped them; Independents under the Constituent Assembly; Terrorists under the Jacobins; and, in fine, zealous Bonapartists: they borrowed the mask of all parties, to gain their countenance and favour.

It was thus that, by their perfidious counsels, they induced Bonaparte to undertake the unjust expedition against Hayti. It was this faction which, after having forced him to this step, furnished the pecuniary means by the lists of subscriptions which were opened at that period. In short, it was this faction which has made the blood of our fellow-countrymen flow in torrents; it was this faction which instigated the unheard of tortures which we have experienced; tortures so frightful as could be devised by none but the colonists, hardened by the practice of every species of crime. It is to the colonists that France owes the loss of a numerous army, which met its fate in the plains and morasses of Hayti; it is to them that she owes the shame of an enterprise which has imprinted an indelible stain on the name of Frenchmen.

We are persuaded, after the cruel experience that we have had of the spirit which animates these colonists, these dealers and traffickers in human flesh, and their vile satellites, that they will once more employ their usual artifices to involve the French cabinet in a new enterprize against us.

If ever this enterprize take place, which we can hardly bring ourselves to believe, it is to this cast, the enemies of the human race; that we shall be indebted for it; for we are very far from imputing to the Europeans, who can have no idea of the colonial system, of which we have been the victims, the dreadful evils we have endured. What interest could the French people have in carrying war into the heart of a nation which was proud of its subjection to them? What interest had they in coming to bury themselves in our destructive climate, and to render themselves the tools and instruments of the colonists, and to sate the thirst of riches and vengeance which inflames them?

However, the majority of the people began to take up arms for the preservation of their lives and liberties from hazard: this first movement spread alarm among the French, and appeared sufficiently serious to General Leclerc, to cause him to convoke an extraordinary assembly of the colonists, in order to adopt measures best calculated to restore a better state of things; but these colonists, very far from relaxing in their atrocious principles, from the imperious sense of danger, unanimously replied in these words, " No slavery, no colony."

As a member of this council, in vain we raised our voice to stop the completion of the ruin of our fellow-countrymen and of our country; in vain did we represent the excessive injustice of replunging free men into slavery; in vain, apprised of the spirit of our countrymen, their love of liberty, we denounced this measure as the only means of ruining the country, and detaching it from France for ever: all was to no purpose. Convinced that there remained no hopes of conciliation, that we must choose between—the bonds of slavery and death—with arms in our hands, we undeceived our fellow-citizens, who had their eyes fixed upon us; and took to arms in obedience to the unanimous impulse, with the resolution to expel our tyrants for ever from our territory, to conquer or die.

General Leclerc had already announced the reduction of the island, and even received, from almost every maritime town in France (where the advocates of the slave trade mostly resided) letters of congratulation on the pretended conquest of Hayti, and the restoration of slavery. Ashamed at having given rise to delusive expectations, chagrined at his inability to execute his detestable enterprise, and dreading the approach of a terrible war, despair consumed his days, and hurried him to the tomb.

Among the catalogue of crimes which signalised the administration of General Leclerc, his conduct to the Haytian General, Maurepas, would excite indignation in hearts least accessible to pity—Maurepas, a man of mild and gentle manners, esteemed for his integrity by his fellow-citizens, was one of the first to surrender to the French, and had rendered them signal services; yet this man was suddenly carried off to Port-de-Paix, and put on board the Admiral's vessel, then riding at anchor in the Cape roads, where, after binding him to the main-mast, they, in derision, fixed with nails such as are used in ship-building, two old epaulettes on his shoulders, and an old general's hat on his head. In that frightful condition, these cannibals, after having glutted their ferocious mirth and exultation, precipitated him with his wife and children into the sea: such was the catastrophe of that virtuous and unfortunate soldier.

To the command of Leclerc succeeded Rochambeau. This monstrous agent of Bonaparte, a worthy accomplice of the colonists, stained himself with every crime, sparing neither sex, nor infancy, nor age; he surpassed in cruelty the most accomplished villains of ancient or modern times. Gibbets were everywhere erected, drownings, burnings; the most horrible punishments were put in practice by his orders; instead of scuttled vessels, he invented a new machine of destruction, in which victims of both sexes, heaped upon one another, were suffocated by wholesale in the smoke of sulphur.

In his insensate rage, he procured from Cuba, at a great expense, human bloodhounds, under charge of one Noailles, of an illustrious French family (who was the first after the Revolution to betray his benefactors), and the human race was delivered to be devoured by dogs that will partake of the frightful immortality of their masters. What was our crime? What had we done to deserve such a proscription? What! must our African original be an eternal opprobrium? Must the colour of our epidermis be the seal of our eternal degradation?

According to the exact return made by order of the government, during the space of twenty-one months that the French resided in this island, more than 16,000 of our fellow-countrymen have perished under the tortures we have specified. The cruelties inflicted by these modern conquerors upon the children of Hayti, blotted out the crimes of the Pizarros, the Cortez, the Bodavillas, those early scourges of the New World.

In spite of all their efforts, we have succeeded in expelling these oppressors from our soil.

To guarantee ourselves for ever from the return of such barbarities, and unheard of crimes, to protect ourselves from similar perfidy and injustice, we resolved to throw off for ever the yoke of foreign domination. In pursuance of this resolution, on the 1st of January 1804, in a general assembly of the national representatives, the independence of Hayti was solemnly proclaimed, and we pronounced the oath to die free and independent, and never again to submit to any foreign domination whatsoever.

Like other people, our first years were not exempt from error and trouble; like them we passed through the vicissitudes inseparable from revolutions.

Since our accession to the throne, our first object has been to elevate the name and dignity of the people of Hayti; convinced that good faith, candour, and probity, in our dealings, the inviolability of property, and personal rights of men, could alone attain that end in our internal and external relations; fully persuaded that it is the laws which constitute the happiness of men united in society, our first measure has been the compiling of a code of laws suitable to our usages, our climate, and our manners. After assiduous application, with the inspiration and assistance of the Almighty, we have at length put the finishing hand to this basis of our social edifice.

We have constantly fostered and protected agriculture and commerce, the channels of public prosperity; abundant harvests have been the fruit of the toilsome exertions of our industrious cultivators; a considerable quantity of produce has been exported from our harbours since we proclaimed our independence, and particularly in the years 1812, 1813, and 1814, by foreign nations, who carry on a traffic with us as safe as it is lucrative.

While directing an anxious inquiry into the measures capable of reviving internal prosperity, we have never diverted our attention from the events which were passing in Europe, in the bloody struggle that she has had to sustain, nor have we ever lost sight, for one instant, of our system of military defence.

In this attitude we waited till Bonaparte, that enemy of the world, should come to attack us, and with his usual weapons, perfidy and force; not forgetting that, after the peace of Amiens, his first object was the famous expedition for our extermination.

But the God of battles, who raises up and casts down thrones at his nod, in his justice, has not willed that this oppressor of nations should accomplish this horrible design. We trust that his fall will give peace and repose to the world; we hope that the return of those liberal and sound principles which animate the European powers will bring them to acknowledge the independence of a people who ask for nothing but to enjoy peace and commerce, which are the chief aims of all civilised nations.

It is in vain to attempt, once more, by means of force or seduction, to make us return under a foreign yoke. We are in no danger from the absurd system of deceiving, in order to govern mankind. Instructed by experience, we come to the knowledge of truth, of reason, and of our own strength ; and the clouds of prejudice, in which our enemies would enwrap and beguile us, are vanished for ever.

We can no more be the victims of our credulity and of good faith ; we can never forget that an attempt has once been made upon our liberty. The heart-rending image of the horrible torments which have precipitated our fathers, our mothers, our wives, our children, into the tomb, shall never be effaced from our memory.

We are no longer open to deception : the underhand practices of our enemies have been made known to us ; we have before our eyes the memoirs and the projects of Malouet, Barré de Saint-Venaut, of the Pages and the Brulleys, and the many other colonists ; the political creed of these brokers of human flesh, these counsellors of evil, is well known to us. It is comprised in two words, *slavery* and *destruction :* we are not ignorant of the criminal intrigues and the shameful practices of those apostles of crime and falsehood ; they have taught us by their writings, more than by the tortures that we have undergone, that the only solid guarantee of our political rights, of our very existence, is the preservation of our independence.

We appeal to all the Sovereigns of the world, to the brave and loyal British nation, which has been the first to proclaim, in its august Senate, the abolition of the infamous traffic in Negroes; which has done still more, in employing the ascendancy of victory for the noble purpose of recommending the abolition to all other states with which she has concluded alliances; we appeal to the philanthropists of all nations; in fine, to mankind at large, to the whole universe, what people, after twenty-five years of battle and bloodshed, having won their liberty and independence with the sword, will ever consent to lay down their arms, and become again the sport and the victims of their cruel oppressors? We ask, what people would stoop to such an excess of baseness? No, the last of the Haytians will breathe out his last sigh before he will renounce his independence.

We will not do any power the injustice to suppose it capable of forming the chimerical hope of establishing its authority in Hayti by the force of arms.

The power that should undertake this enterprize, would have to march a long time over ruins and carcases ; and if, after having displayed all its means, it should at length make itself master of the country, after burying the flower of its troops, which yet we hold to be impossible, what will it have purchased with the loss of so much treasure, with the effusion of so much blood?

It would not be presumptuous to believe that his Majesty, Louis XVIII. following the impulse of the philanthropic spirit which has ever reigned in his family, and imitating the example of his unfortunate brother, Louis XVI. in his political conduct towards the United States of America, will tread in the steps of that monarch, and acknowledge the independence of Hayti. It would be but an act of justice, a poor amends for the evils we have suffered under the government of France.

It is in vain that our detractors dare still to allege, that *we must not be considered as a political body aspiring to independence, and collectively occupied in the means to obtain it.**

This absurd assertion, invented by the craft, the wickedness, and base selfishness of the advocates of the Slave Trade, merits the most profound contempt and indignation of the good men of all countries ; and is sufficiently belied by eleven years' actual enjoyment of independence and its happy results. There is no example of a people that have made so rapid a progress in civilization.

Free by right, and independent in fact, we will never renounce these blessings; no, never will we consent to see subverted the edifice we have raised and cemented by

* Introduction to the Memoirs of St. Domingo. MALONET, vol. iv. p. 56.

our blood ; at least, without being buried beneath its ruins.

To the commercial powers inclined to connect themselves with us, we offer our friendship, the security of their property, and our royal protection to their peaceable subjects, who may land upon our shores with the intention of pursuing their commercial affairs, and conform with our laws and customs.

King of a free people, a soldier by profession, we dread not war, nor the enemy with which we may have to fight; we have already declared our resolution not to intermeddle, in any manner, in the internal government of our neighbours ; we wish to enjoy, at home, peace and tranquillity, and to exercise the universal prerogative of making such laws for ourselves as our exigencies require. If, after the frank exposure of our sentiments and of the justice of our cause, a hostile foot shall plant itself upon our territory, in violation of the rights of nations, our first duty will then be to repel the act of aggression by every means in our power.

We solemnly declare, that we will never become a party to any treaty, to any condition, that may compromise the honour, the liberty, or the independence of the Haytian people; that, true to our oath, we will sooner bury ourselves beneath the ruins of our native country, than suffer an infraction of our political rights.

Given at our palace of Sans Souci, the 18th of September, 1814, in the 11th year of independence, and the 4th of our reign.

HENRY.

(By the King)

Comte de LIMONADE,

Secretary of State, Minister of Foreign Affairs.

From Sans Souci, the 3d January,
1816.

THE anniversary of the festival of our immortal independence (written from the above city) has been celebrated with the greatest pomp during two days.

The day before, at sun-set, and the day after, at the first break of morn, salvos of artillery saluted the beautiful day of independence.

At seven o'clock the five superb regiments of the household troops of the king, in the closest order, and the different corps of the garrison, filed off from their barracks to repair to the exercising ground.

At eight o'clock, the dignitaries and grand officers assembled, went to the palace of His Royal Highness the Prince Royal, generalissimo of the army, to form his retinue, and accompany him to the ground.

The whole marched off to the sound of drums and music. On reaching the place of exercise, his Royal Highness ordered the manœuvre of forming the troops in column to be performed, and desired the populace to approach, in order to hear read the Act of Independence and the Proclamation of the King.

The Chevalier de Prézeau, secretary to the King, read aloud the Act of Independence, and at the termination of it, cries of " Independence for ever !" were heard in all quarters.

Then Baron de Vastey read aloud the Proclamation of the King, which carried enthusiasm to its height, and was equally received with cries of " Independence for ever ! Long live the King ! Liberty for ever !"

These readings being finished, his Royal Highness repaired with his retinue to the palace of the King, his august father, to pay him his respectful homage.

The dignitaries, civil and administrative officers, were introduced by the grand master of the ceremonies in the great saloon, and ranked according to the order of precedence. Immediately after the King made his appearance, having on each side the Queen, the Prince Royal, and the Princesses Royal.

Baron Dessalines, major general, the Organ of the Peers, advanced respectfully, and addressed the King in the following speech :

SIRE,

To offer to your Majesty and your august family, on the anniversary of the immortal independence of our country, the tribute of our respectful homage, of our veneration, our fidelity and unbounded devotion, is to discharge the debt of our hearts unto your Majesty, as the pledge of our gratitude.

The wisdom of your Majesty's administration claims the affection of all Haytians, the esteem and admiration of foreigners. Sire, your Majesty had scarcely concluded the preparations for the defence of our country; your profound discernment had scarcely provided for all that is morally possible to foresee in the safety of the people, when your Majesty, entertaining the noble idea of raising up the character of the nation, engaged in the introduction of knowledge into the kingdom, as the means of civilizing man.—You are desirous, Sire, of uniting with the sublime institutions which you have given us, and of adding to justice and morality, which have made such rapid progress amongst us, the arts and sciences, those amiable offsprings of peaceable times!

All your Majesty's thoughts, all your desires, invoke among us unison and peace. The Haytian people do that justice to your Majesty which is but due, that, if all the districts of Haytians are not yet reunited, your Majesty has nevertheless done all in your power in order to accomplish this most gratifying end ; but, what must be consolatory to the beneficent heart of your Majesty is, that its paternal advances have not been thrown away. Already the majority of our brethren, who have been hurried on in error by a vile and ambitious man who has sacrificed all, are now about to open their eyes to the light of conviction, and to reunite themselves under the banners of your Majesty, which are those of their own proper cause, of liberty and independence.

Pursue, Sire, your glorious destinies : may you ever be to the Haytians that great guide which is to direct their steps in the new career they are about to commence ; the compass by which to steer our warriors in the paths of honour and glory, as well as in the practice of the duty of a good father, good husband, and good Haytian! your Majesty will find in your own heart the sweetest recompence for all your troubles, for all your toils and works that are imperishable.

Permit, Sire, your officers to wish you all the happiness and blessings of which your Majesty is so worthy. May the Supreme Being preserve you many years to be the support of the country, and the consternation of our tyrants.

Long live the King! Independence for ever!

His Majesty received the address of the dignitaries and peers very graciously, and replied in the following terms:

SIRS, Dignitaries and Officers of the civil and administrative bodies,—It is with the most lively acknowledgments that we receive the wishes you express on our behalf at the commencement of this new year. Penetrated with the sincerity of those wishes, we receive them with the most profound regard. You will learn by our Proclamation of this day, the state of the prosperity of the kingdom, and our views of augmenting its renown. All our power shall be exerted to advance the happiness of the people; their felicity, their reputation, shall ever be the object of our constant solicitude, and the end of our unceasing vigilance and toil.

By promoting amongst you union, which creates strength, under the regulation of the laws; by practising good conduct, and the observance of justice and of equity; by fostering and encouraging the arts and sciences, so as to attract the consideration and good-will of friendly powers, by our wisdom, our good faith, and the security of our trade; by our warlike attitude, and our steady resolution; let us render ourselves worthy of liberty and independence! May these sublime

sentiments be engraven on our hearts!
Such, gentlemen, is the end to which all
our views and endeavours are directed;
and this same sun that illumes with its
beneficent rays the day we are celebrating,
will rise ever beaming on us, and our posterity!

The ceremony being over, the Prince
and Princesses Royal got into their car-
riages to go to church, and assist in divine
service.

After mass their Majesties returned to
the palace in the same order in which they
had set out. A splendid entertainment
was served up ; the utmost gaiety prevailed during the repast, and after dinner,
during the dessert, patriotic toasts were
given and received with loud acclamations, followed by music, the flourish of
trumpets, and salutes of cannon.

At night the palace and city were illu-
minated in the most brilliant manner ; a

grand ball was given at the palace. The two days of rejoicing to commemorate our immortal independence were passed in the most pleasing enjoyments : never was the court more brilliantly attended : the unanimity, freedom, and gaiety that prevailed, were proofs of the unbounded attachment which the Haytians feel for their liberty and their independence.

REFLECTIONS

OF

THE EDITOR.

THE greatest happiness of a nation is that of possessing a wise and valiant King, who knows how to make his rights respected abroad, and who studies the internal administration of his laws with justice and equity: this happiness we possess: we have, in our beloved Sovereign, this wise and valiant monarch: it is he who by his energy and his courage knows how to cause our liberty and independence to be respected: it is he who by the wisdom of his administration has attracted towards us the admiration and esteem of strangers: he it is who has amended our manners, fixed our institutions and our laws, and who is still further desirous, to complete his benefits to the full, by introducing into the kingdom the lights of learning, by affording his protection to the arts and sciences ; he it is who watches by night and day for the maintenance of our rights ; he observes the plots of Frenchmen and of their partisans, to discomfit them; it is around this wise and valiant King, therefore, my brethren, that we ought all to rally and to fight until our latest breath, in order to establish our rights, our liberty, and our independence !

Why, my brethren, have not all of us this sublime thought ? Why is it that one weak portion of the Haytians still bends under the ignominious yoke of a traitor ? They know not, all the while, the sundry crimes with which Petion is covered : do they wait then till, with their hands and feet bound, they are delivered up, before they will open their eyes ?

Has not Petion renounced real independence in consideration of retaining only one species of independence, the internal administration? has he not bartered away the rights of the people with an infamous spy? would he not have delivered them up to the mercy of their butchers, if he were not apprehensive of risking his safety and his existence? has he not granted the exclusive privilege of trade to France? has he not agreed that he had become Haytian against his will, through necessity, at a time when he could not act otherwise? is it not he who would send the Haytians to the Island of Ratau? is it not he who has furnished Dauxion Lavaysse with all the plans and designs for a conquest, to reduce us to a state of slavery? Finally, is it not he who is perpetually conspiring abroad and at home in favour of the French? Meronet, Garbage, Tapiant, Liott, Dauxion Lavaysse, Catineau Laroche, the two brothers Pradert, are not these his agents and his ac-

complices? I should never finish in re-
counting the history of all his crimes.
Blind must that man be who serves such
a monster.

We feel a great curiosity to learn in
what manner Petion has kept the anniversary of independence at Port au Prince,
he who had already sacrificed it, who
carried his repugnance to it so far as not
to be desirous of pronouncing the word or
inserting it in his writings : but as this
hypocrite often sings his recantation according to circumstances, it is probable
he will have observed the day with much
ceremony, to mask his criminal intentions,
in order, if possible, to dispel the recollection of his intrigues with Dauxion
Lavaysse.

We are informed that, for some time
past, he affects in his conversation to
speak against the French, with a view to
attempt to regain that popularity which
his treason forfeited ; but every one se-

cretly derides him; no one is the dupe of his fresh juggles; and they are right; for a traitor is ever to be mistrusted.

We also learn from London, that M. Lainé and M. the Duke de Lewis, two violent ex-colonists, fill the highest situations about Louis XVIII.: these two gentlemen, governed by the same views as the late Malonet, will not fail to make, with Petion, a new league against the liberty and independence of the Haytian people.

Two vessels of war, it is said, have sailed from France with commissioners to confer with Petion; we enjoin our citizens of the west and southern provinces to have their eyes open to watch Petion's conduct with that of the white Frenchmen, and not to allow themselves to be deceived by this traitor as before; if they have still the insolence to threaten you, to treat you as offending savages, and to entrap you, as the negroes, to be subservient to their own purposes, seize

them as well as that traitor Petion; deliver them over to us, that they may share
the destiny of that spy Feanco Medina,
who is their accomplice!

ROYAL GAZETTE OF HAYTI.

4th JANUARY 1816,

Thirteenth Year of Independence.

UNION CREATES STRENGTH.

From Cape Henry the 3d January
1816, the Year 13.

ALL the nations of the earth have had re-
markable æras, to which they have attached
the greatest celebrity: in order to perpetuate
the remembrance of benefits they have received, they have instituted festivals and public
recreations wherein they might indulge the
effusions of their hearts. Religion, the wisdom
of states, has consecrated these customs.

It is in these public festivals that the national spirit displays itself, the enthusiasm that reigns in the heart is the certain testimony of affection and attachment in the people to that object which is the cause of the general rejoicing. Having thus premised, we shall proceed to notice the anniversary of our immortal Independence which has just been celebrated throughout the kingdom with more pomp and magnificence than ever!

Indeed, what epoch should be more glorious for Haytians than the aniversary of their Independence, the sole guarantee of their political and individual existence? Memorable is the day on which we burst and broke in pieces our chains! Great and glorious is this day, on which, restored to our true dignity, we have sworn to posterity, to the whole universe, ever to renounce France, and to die sooner than exist under its dominion.

Before publishing the details of the festival, we will lay before our readers the Proclamation of the King, our august and beloved Sovereign, the defender of our rights, the chief and firmest support of our liberty and of our Independence.

Kingdom of Hayti.

PROCLAMATION.

THE KING TO THE HAYTIANS.

HAYTIANS!

THIS is the sacred day, for ever memorable, on which we proclaimed in the face of the universe, our firm and unalterable resolution, to live free and independent, or to die. Liberty and Independence! How do these words recall to us great and glorious recollections! to what sublime sentiments do they give rise in our minds, and how ought we to cherish these precious benefits, the prize of our constancy and our valour, purchased by the purest of our blood!

Our first thought on this great day is to offer up our thanks to Divine Providence for the full measure of his benefits poured out upon us, in releasing us from the state of ignominy and misery into which we were plunged, to restore us to a state of society, civilization, and to happiness.

This first duty being fulfilled, there remains for us a second, very dear to our paternal heart, which is that of laying before you the situation of the kingdom in an explanation of the results of our labours for the past year; you will perceive our state of existing prosperity, and we shall make known to you our views of introducing into the kingdom the arts and sciences, to encourage and protect them, to make them flourish, and to employ and combine all those measures of wisdom which can contribute to the happiness and prosperity of the Haytian people.

Relying with confidence on your unremitting and generous efforts, we are fully convinced that you will contribute at all times to second us in the execution of our projects, and that you will apply to them the same zeal, the same ardour, of which we have received so many proofs, particularly in the year which has just elapsed.

Resolved never to interfere but in matters that concern us, solely occupied with the care of ameliorating our internal situation, and consolidating, by institutions and by laws, the edifice of our liberty and of our independence; in 1814 we were menaced with an unjust aggression; the French, instead of enjoying like other nations the advantages and sweets of that peace which they had just obtained of the High Allies, instead of applying themselves like them to healing the evils of war, instead of making some amends for their cruelties and injuries to us, by a conduct more humane and diametrically opposite, at first, attempted again to revive their odious pretensions, and to disturb us in the peaceful enjoyment of our rights; pretensions equally unjust, chimerical, and barbarous, devoid of every kind of foundation and of reason! Pretensions as vain, as erroneous, as those which would arrogate to us the kingdom of France!

Our posterity will not have to reproach us for having been wanting in all that our honour, our country, our dearest interests prescribed to us; we have replied to their new outrages with the firmness and energy that characterize us, and thus will we ever repel all unjust pretensions, all propositions offered in contempt of our liberty and of our independence.

Our existence as a nation and as individuals being menaced, the year 1815 was employed in making preparations for war; our system of defence was wholly completed; our citadels were finished, perfected, and stocked with provisions and warlike stores; the army kept constantly on the war-footing, was again considerably increased, skeleton corps were filled up complete, new regiments were raised, the militias of the kingdom were newly organized in a manner more suitable to our localities, and to their destinations; the troops of the line were clothed, equipped, and provided with new musquets; the royal Dahomets clothed and equipped themselves voluntarily at their own cost and expense; we have decorated with the cross of our order many brave officers of this corps as the reward of their zeal, and the eminent services which they have never ceased to render to their country.

Good order and discipline prevail among the troops of every description; they are constantly exercised in the manœuvres; our preparations of war are finished; the whole population is armed; our magazines are provided with necessaries to maintain a long war, without desiring it, without provoking it, without fearing it: confiding in the most just of causes, the future has nothing in it that can alarm us: we may look it in the face with security.

Our finances are in a satisfactory state. Without bordering on parsimony, the receipts of the current year have been sufficient to keep pace with the enormous expenditure to which our state of war has unavoidably given rise.

Entirely warriors and agriculturists by nature, notwithstanding our military preparations we have never ceased to entertain a solicitude for cultivation, the fundamental basis of our riches, that source from which flow the power and prosperity of the kingdom.

Commerce has continued to be most lucrative. We are abundantly provided with objects of consumption imported into the country. Numerous vessels of friendly powers have effected the sale of their cargoes in our ports, and sailed again richly laden with commodities. Agriculture, that principal source of our national prosperity, will increase still progressively by the impulse we give to it, and by the encouragements and privileges granted to the inhabitants of the country. Commerce, intimately connected by its relations with the success of agriculture, will augment itself equally by the profits, the protection, the security of persons, and of property, which we grant to foreign merchants who trade with us.

Population increases by degrees: the happiness of which the different classes of society partake, is the sure guarantee of its increase.

The laws are regularly executed; the magistrates fulfil their duties; justice is exercised with scrupulous exactness; the people daily acquire the knowledge of their rights and of their duties; their public spirit is excellent; it is impossible to deceive them respecting their true interests.

History informs us that all nations, prior to their civilization, were sunk in the darkness of barbarism: it is only after the lapse of a consi-

derable time that they civilize themselves by
the introduction of knowledge, the effect of instruction and of time. With a view to discharge
that prime duty in the administration of a state,
public instruction has particularly engaged our
attention : we have sought from abroad for
learned professors and skilful artists of every
kind, in order to introduce into the kingdom
the arts and sciences.

The professors and artists who shall establish themselves here for the purpose of undertaking the instruction of youth, shall be particularly encouraged and protected; they will
experience the utmost toleration : difference of
nation and religion will be no ground of exclusion : we shall pay respect to merit and talents alone. The virtuous man, without any
regard to the country that may have given him
birth, or the faith in which he may have been
brought up, shall always meet a kind reception,
and shall enjoy the advantages of protection
and security which our laws impart to strangers
of all nations who inhabit the kingdom.

The places of education, the colleges, the
royal and military school, will become the nur-

sery from whence are to issue our statesmen, magistrates of enlightened character, and military men instructed in the art of war.

During the completion of our plans, we have given orders for making a constant progress in the construction of buildings necessary for the public establishments in the towns and in the country.

The situation of the kingdom at large is such as to present us only with matter of satisfaction. We are arrived at the summit of our wishes, since at the commencement of this new year, we have the sweet satisfaction of announcing to you the total extinction of civil war.

This species of insanity, this fury of passions which had been kindled in some hearts, is visibly extinguished: already a part of the people in the southern province have ranged themselves under our standard, and the rest are ready to unite with our brave companions who have embraced the cause of legitimate authority, of liberty, and independence. What do I say? It is their own cause. We are also assured that the Haytians of the western portion are like-

wise ready to imitate the good example of our
fellow-countrymen of the south.

Sovereign of the nation, our paternal affection extends equally over all Haytians.
From the south to the north, from the east to
the west, all parts of the terr'tory form the integrity of our kingdom; all its inhabitants
have therefore equal claim to the benevolence
of the King of Hayti; for we have already repeated, and we repeat it again, that we do not
consider ourselves as king over a portion of the
territory, or of a part of the population, but of
all the kingdom, and of the whole people.
Those who have been hurried on in error and
misfortune by an ambitious man, are much
more to be pitied than blamed; a day will
come, and that day is not distant, when they
will discover their errors; then will they rival
us in order to consolidate the rights and liberty,
and independence of our country.

Resolved never to be diverted from our
pacific system, just and liberal as it is, the only
one that accords with our paternal heart, and
the general interests of the people, and satisfied
with the good intentions displayed by the in-

habitants of the southern province, we have sent back to their homes the troops of that part which happened to be in our ranks through the events of the war, in order that they may defend them, and in testimony of their good conduct, and of the zeal which animates them for the good of our service. The sailors and inhabitants of that province which have fallen into our hands have been well treated, and kindly received by our orders : those who have manifested a desire to return to their homes have been sent back to the bosom of their families.

Haytians ! such is the exposition. of our internal situation. Our situation improves every day. Held in consideration without, and within, we assume a respectable attitude. The military art which defends the country is brought to perfection. The social virtues which form good fathers of families, good sons, and chaste spouses, are practised. Religion is reverenced ; our manners become refined ; the conjugal tie is respected ; the odious vices, the offspring of ignorance and of a barbarous thraldrom, sensibly disappear, or are obliged to hide themselves in darkness. The protection afforded to marriage, the decay of vice, with the shame that is attached to it, ensure the progress of morality, which with the difference of knowledge, concurs powerfully to our attainment of a degree of civilization at which the most polished nations of the earth have arrived.

Haytians! twenty-six years of revolution unparalleled in the history of the world, thirteen of the independence so gloriously acquired, have effected wonders! No, we are no longer the same men! What prodigious changes have been effected in every thing that surrounds us! Formerly the dejected countenance—the look fixed upon the ground—assimilated to the brutes—and oppressed under the scourge of the tormenter, we nevertheless existed, though extinct as to the world. We had faculties, yet these faculties were annihilated under the load of servitude and of ignorance! The cry of liberty made itself heard, and suddenly we broke our irons into pieces. With a countenance erect, and the look fixed upon Heaven, we could contemplate the works of Divine munificence! Restored to the dignity of man, and to society, we acquired a new existence, our faculties developed themselves, a career of happiness and of glory unfolds itself before us! Mighty God! Supreme arbiter of the universe, thanksgiving be ever rendered unto thee! Accept the solemn vows and adoration we offer up to thee! Virtuous philanthropists! friends of humanity! contemplate the work of your hands, the fruit of your labour and your toils, still redouble, if it be possible, your zeal and ardour to establish the happiness of the human race! the Haytians will justify your generous efforts by their deeds and memorable examples!

Henceforth the calumniators of the human species will have to argue by sophisms, and by cases of exception; instead of replying to them, we will make rapid strides towards civilization. Let them dispute, if they please, the existence of our intellectual faculties, our little or no aptness for the arts and sciences, whilst we reply to these by irresistible arguments, and prove to the impious, by facts and by examples, that the blacks, like the whites, are men, and like them are the works of a Divine Omnipotence!

Generals, officers, subalterns and soldiers
by land and by sea, Royal Dahomets, magistrates, inhabitants of the towns and of the
country, receive our congratulations for the
zeal and ardour you have exerted in seconding
our preparations for the defence of our country,
your generous devotion and patriotism deserve
our gratitude and the acknowledgments of the
country!

You have proved to the world, that all
manner of sacrifices are to you as nothing, when
the maintenance of those rights which you
derive from God, from nature, and from justice, is called in question; persevere always
in these sublime sentiments, and you will be
invincible; contemn, disdain that which pusillanimous men may value, Life and Fortune.
You Haytians, your true interests, without
which, all the others are as nought, are Liberty and Independence!

Our tyrants overwhelmed with the same
weight of calamity with which they had afflicted the Universe, are compelled to leave
us quiet. Once victims of our good faith and
our credulity, let us never forget, that the first

use they made of the last peace was to endeavour to deceive us a second time in the most
perfidious manner. Can we again suffer ourselves to be so deceived? Which is he among
us who would renounce his birthright as a man,
to return to the condition of the brute, under
the yoke of tyrants? The very idea fills us
with horror, and makes the breast to heave with
indignation! .... They may frame new plots,
they may metamorphose themselves in a thousand shapes; no Haytians, no, never will we
fall into the snares which they may spread
for us!

Haytians! we have not to labour for our
own happiness alone, we labour still for our
posterity. Let us impress our minds with the
sacred duties we have to discharge towards
ourselves, and those in like situations; we have
given our enemies the most striking proofs of
resolution, energy, and courage; but this is
not enough, we have another species of con-
test to wage with them. Henceforth, it is by
the wisdom of our laws, the purity of our
manners, our virtues, the security of our commerce, our constant efforts and laborious toils

for the prosperity of our country, that we will prove to them we are worthy of Liberty and Independence !

Liberty for ever !
Independence for ever !

Given in our Royal Palace of Sans-Souci, the 1st January, 1816. The thirteenth year of independence, and of our reign the fifth.

HENRY.

By the King, the Secretary of State,
Minister of Foreign Affairs,

COUNT LIMONADE.

REFLECTIONS

ON THE

ABOLITION OF THE SLAVE TRADE.

Among the great events that tend to adorn the Calendar of the nineteenth century, the Abolition of the Slave Trade, that odious and blood-stained traffic, deserves to rank the first in history, while the names of those generous characters who have effected it, will be handed down to posterity as the benefactors of the human race!

God, whose infinite wisdom governs all earthly things by decrees that are to us inscrutable, for the accomplishment of his all-wise purposes, raised up that terrible Revolution which shook the Universe; he laid the weight of his mighty hand over Potentates and nations to punish the inconsiderateness of their hearts. Established thrones were overturned, others endangered, while Monarchs were led into captivity, or compelled as exiles to fly for security to a foreign land, and not even the Head of the Catholic Church was exempt. Europe, the oppressor of Africa and America, saw itself in turn covered with crimes and inundated with the blood of her own Sons.

Of this Revolution, a terrible dispensation of Divine Providence, undertaken by men with very different designs, what is now the result? The freedom of nations !

When the French coalition operated with so much zeal for the destruction of England, could it ever have imagined that it was only the instrument of her glory and prosperity?

The supreme Arbiter of the Universe had decreed in his immutable judgments, that the powerful and generous nation which was to stem in its course the torrent that was devastating Europe, and to rescue her from the brink of the precipice, was also to be the first to stretch its succouring and protecting hand to the oppressed people of Africa and America.

Noble and generous England, by the wis-

dom of its government is become the mediatrix
of the world, and the common tie which is to
unite all nations !

Moreover, this great country enjoys eternal
glory, as the reward of the services she has
rendered to the human race, whilst other nations who have persisted in closing their hearts
to every claim of justice and humanity, are
stamped with signs of degeneracy, and calamities of every kind are afflicting their territories.

How many favours do we owe to the magnanimous and illustrious Sovereigns of England,
of Russia, and of Germany, for their having
insisted upon the abolition of that traffic !

How many acknowledgements does every
man of Black origin owe to those venerable
and illustrious philanthropists of THE AFRICAN
INSTITUTION ! Never did any society devote
itself to the protection of a cause more holy and
more just; never have true Christians defended, more charitably, more benignantly, and
at the same time more zealously for humanity,
the cause of mankind, than our distinguished
patrons have done; how many crimes and

transgressions are about to be banished from
the earth, through the intervention, the vigilance, and laborious exertions of these generous
men! Desolated Africa will no longer see her
unhappy sons carried off from her shores: no
longer shall they be torn from the embraces
of their family, by all kinds of artifices, or of
crimes to be doomed to perpetual slavery on a
foreign soil! The *Brokes,* those infernal slave
ships, shall exist no more; we shall no more behold those receptacles of sin, of which the
very sight fills one with horror, and speaks to
the heart more than the eloquence of volumes
could convey! No longer shall our brethren be
heaped up in those moving dungeons, loaded
with chains, and overwhelmed with grief—I
stop: let me pause to recover myself. Sentiments of indignation crowd upon me; tears of
pity and acknowledgment flow from the recital! Worthy and benevolent men! Continue
that task you have so nobly undertaken, and
you will carry in your own hearts the recompence of your good deeds.

A new æra arises for Africa under the protecting shield of philanthropic men: its inha-

bitants may breathe in the bosom of their country the pure air of liberty ; they may enjoy the sweets and advantages of civilization in devoting themselves to the cultivation of the earth, to the pursuits of commerce, of science, and of art : we even indulge the hope that, one day or other, they may revive, by their labours, the recollection of our illustrious ancestors.

In the irresistible march of the affairs of this world, every thing paints the instability of sublunary concerns : empires rise and fall, flourish and decay. The light of knowledge follows the impulse of revolutions, and travels, successively, over the surface of the globe. Greece, Germany, and Gaul, were not originally the seats of learning. Our traducers pretend to have forgotten what the Egyptians and Ethiopians, our ancestors, were : the Tharaca of Scripture, that mighty monarch who was the dread of the Assyrians, came from the interior of Africa, as far as the columns of Hercules, the records that attest their works, still remain : the testimony of Herodotus, of Strabo, and of other historians of antiquity, confirm these facts. More recent proofs bear evidence in our favour, and yet our enemies, with signal incredulity, feign to doubt all this, in order to preserve to themselves the odious privilege of torturing, and persecuting, according to their own will, one portion of the human race.

These false Christians, foes to God and to humanity, assert that we are of a lower scale of being than the whites: many among them have been so impious as to deny the identity of the human species, and absurd enough to affirm that we are on a level with the brutes, deprived of moral and intellectual faculties.

Our friends, the true Christians, maintain that we are endowed with intellect, that our natural capacities are good, and that they would be equal to those of Europeans if we had the same advantages: they regard us as their brethren, *for the Deity hath created, of one blood, the whole human race, to dwell over every part of the earth.*

It were easy for us to reply to our traducers, and to prove the truth of the assertions advanced by our patrons. In all ages of the world there have existed impious and sophistical men; sceptics too, who deny the existence of God, and of free agency; to answer whom philosophers have only to change places; we may do the same, and so reply to our enemies as victoriously.

Let us devote ourselves to the cultivation of letters, of arts and sciences, which develope intellect; let us store our minds with principles of morality and wisdom; let us redouble our zeal and ardour to annihilate calumny, and dispel the prejudices that hover over us; and soon shall we have, like other nations, by our liberal endeavours, our senate house, our heroes, our legislators, our historians, our poets, our painters, our sculptors, and our learned men.

Placed by Divine Providence in a situation, and amid circumstances more favourable than our ancestors, we can more easily than they make rapid strides in the career of civilization : let us then always bear in mind, that we are the elect, whom God hath chosen from among so many of our brethren who groan in slavery, to manifest to mankind, by living examples, that the Blacks are, like the Whites, the work of his hands, and Almighty Power.

We should understand that we labour for the benefit of the human race generally, for the Black equally as for the White ; for we are all brethren : let us recollect that African blood flows in our veins, and that we are under the necessity of exerting our utmost efforts to live in the great practice of society ; our progress more or less influencing the opinions that the Europeans will form of us !

We should understand that we are still sur-rounded with quicksands ; that there are no intrigues, or schemes, or artifices which the French Ex-colonists or their partisans will leave unemployed to obstruct the bark of li-berty and independence on its arrival at the destined haven : there are no subtleties or abo-minations which they will omit in order to fetter its progress. O horrible criminality ! they were not ashamed to propose sending Catholic Priests, Apostolics, and Romans, in order first to seduce, under the venerable garb of religion, our population, and then to sink it by degrees into the horrors of slavery ! O abomination ! O sa-crilegious conduct ! The ministers of the God of peace and of charity have dared to become the willing instruments of the passions, the vengeance and barbarity of French Ex-colonists!! Descendants of Africans, my brethren, the friends of humanity have asserted that we are susceptible of improvement like the Whites; our traducers affirm the contrary; it is for us to decide the question; it is by the wisdom of our conduct, our success in the arts and sciences, that we shall secure the triumph of our respected and illustrious patrons, and confound, for ever, the malice and unfounded assertions of our implacable enemies.

The Deity hath granted us all that is wanting to accomplish this generous design, in having rendered us free and independent, and in bestowing upon us a wise and liberal Monarch, who is ever vigilant to administer to our wants. We are aware of his great and good intentions; he has always manifested them towards us: what he has already effected is the sure guarantee of what he can still do for the happiness and glory of the people. Ah! what might he not have done, had he been seconded by the generality of Haytians? Why will one portion of our fellow-citizens be deceived by the seduction of a hypocrite, a traitor won over to their purposes by the Ex-colonists, endeavouring to demoralize the nation, in order to render it subservient to the cause of our tyrants, and finally to succeed in plunging it into an abyss of evils? The very idea makes the heart to bleed, and fills our souls with bitterness : let us hope that our brethren will become sensible of their errors, and that they will return to their true interests, to labour with us in promoting the triumph of the great cause of humanity and of religion.

In concluding our reflections on the Abolition of the Slave Trade, we acquit ourselves of a duty in consecrating here the names of the illustrious members of the AFRICAN INSTITUTION, who have mainly contributed to effect the abolition of this inhuman, criminal, and bloodstained traffic! It is a feeble homage we pay to their immortal labours! May the names of these generous and benevolent characters be engraven on the heart of every Haytian, to be perpetuated from age to age in the recollection of our offspring and of the remotest posterity!

PATRON AND PRESIDENT,

His Highness the DUKE of GLOUCESTER.

VICE PRESIDENTS.

His Grace the Archbishop of Canterbury.
The Most Honourable the Marquis of Lansdown.
The Right Honourable the Earl of Bristol.
The Right Honourable Earl Spencer.
The Right Honourable Earl Grosvenor.
The Right Honourable Earl of Rossyln.
The Right Honourable Earl Grey.
The Right Honourable Earl Moira.
The Right Honourable Earl of Selkirk.
The Right Honourable Earl of Caledon.
The Right Honourable Viscount Milton.
The Right Honourable Viscount Valentia.
The Lord Bishop of Durham.
The Lord Bishop of Bath and Wells.
The Lord Bishop of St. David's.
The Right Honourable Lord Holland.
The Right Honourable Lord Grenville.
The Right Honourable Lord Calthorpe.

The Right Honourable Lord Erskine.

The Right Honourable Lord Gambier,

The Right Honourable Lord Headley.

The Right Honourable Lord Teignmouth.

The Right Honourable George Canning, M. P,

The Right Honourable J. C. Villiers.

The Right Honourable Nicholas Vansittart, M.P.

Sir Samuel Romilly, M. P.

William Wilberforce, Esq. M. P.

DIRECTORS.

The Honourable Capt. F. P. Irby, R. N.

The Honourable George Vernon.

Sir Thomas Bernard, Bart.

Sir John Cradock, K. B.

Sir James Mackintosh, M. P.

Sir Robert Wilson, K. M. T.

William Allen, Esq.

Thomas Babington, Esq. M. P.

Charles Barclay, Esq. M. P.

William Blake, Esq.

Henry Brougham, Esq. M. P.

Thomas Clarkson, Esq.

Colonel Dalton.

Rev. William Dealtry.

Thomas Furley Forster, Esq.

Robert Grant, Esq.

George Harrison, Esq.

Thomas Harrison, Esq.

William Henry Hoare, Esq.

Francis Horner, Esq. M. P.

Zachary Macauley, Esq.

Matthew Martin, Esq.

J. B. S. Marritt, M. P.

Charles Pieschell, Esq.

William Foster Reynolds, Esq.

William Smith, Esq. M. P.

John Henry Smith, Esq. M. P.

Lieutenant-General Stevenson.

James Stephen, Esq.

James Stephen, jun. Esq.

Rev. James Towers.

Henry Warburton, Esq.

John Whishaw, Esq.

Samuel Whitbread, Esq. M. P.

Ed. B. Wilbraham, Esq. M. P.

James Rice Williams, Esq.

AUDITORS.

Thomas Barnett, Esq.

John Mortlock, Esq.

B. M. Forster, Esq.

John Thornton, Esq. Treasurer.

Mr. Robert Stokes, Clerk.

Thomas Harrison, Esq. Secretary.

Messrs. Lambert and Son, Solicitors.

Mr. Abraham Tattet, Collector.

Charles Bala, Messenger.

T. Bensley and Son,
Bolt Court, Fleet Street, London.

For EU product safety concerns, contact us at Calle de José Abascal, 56–1°, 28003 Madrid, Spain or eugpsr@cambridge.org.

www.ingramcontent.com/pod-product-compliance
Ingram Content Group UK Ltd.
Pitfield, Milton Keynes, MK11 3LW, UK
UKHW010340140625
459647UK00010B/721